When Grandpa Delivered Babies
and Other Ozarks Vignettes

WHEN GRANDPA DELIVERED BABIES

and Other Ozarks Vignettes

BENJAMIN G. RADER

UNIVERSITY OF
ILLINOIS PRESS
Urbana, Chicago, and Springfield

© 2024 by the Board of Trustees
of the University of Illinois
All rights reserved
Manufactured in the United States of America
1 2 3 4 5 C P 5 4 3 2 1
∞ This book is printed on acid-free paper.

Library of Congress Cataloging-in-Publication Data
Names: Rader, Benjamin G., author.
Title: When Grandpa delivered babies and other Ozarks
   vignettes / Benjamin G. Rader.
Description: Urbana : University of Illinois Press, [2024] |
   Includes bibliographical references.
Identifiers: LCCN 2023027592 (print) | LCCN 2023027593
   (ebook) | ISBN 9780252045745 (hardback) | ISBN
   9780252087844 (paperback) | ISBN 9780252056604 (ebook)
Subjects: LCSH: Rader, Benjamin G. | Rader family. | Ozark
   Mountains Region—Biography. | Ozark Mountains Region—
   Anecdotes. | Ozark Mountains Region—Social life and
   customs—20th century. | Missouri—Biography. | Missouri—
   Anecdotes. | Missouri—Social life and customs—20th
   century.
Classification: LCC F472.O9 R26 2024 (print) | LCC F472.O9
   (ebook) | DDC 977.8/8092 [B]—dc23
LC record available at https://lccn.loc.gov/2023027592
LC ebook record available at https://lccn.loc.gov/2023027593

CONTENTS

PART IV. ARE WE IN THE OZARKS NOW?

PREFACE

My grandfather Alford "Raz" Eddings was something of a local shaman. Said to have had native ancestry and abetted by his knowledge of roots and herbs, he regularly treated the illnesses of his neighbors. He delivered babies as well. When the time came for his wife, Florence, to give birth, he hung the family's kitchen table oilcloth out on the clothesline. He then ordered his children to go down to McHenry Creek and play. When the birth was completed, he took down the oilcloth. His children then knew that they could return to the house and meet one or more of their new siblings. Witnessing the pains of his wife's childbirth did not deter Raz from the pleasures of the marriage bed. Within two decades of their marriage in 1910, Florence presented him with ten living daughters and one living son plus three children who died in childbirth or shortly thereafter.

Grandpa Raz came to a startling conclusion about one of his daughters. He decided that Iva had in effect murdered her twin sister by denying her food in the womb. Since Iva was therefore a "witch," he refused to permit her baptism. When I learned about this many years later, my mind unaccountably leaped to the conclusion that his decision had something to do with Iva never having had children of her own, although she did have three different husbands. Upon leaving home, Iva forthwith sought out a preacher who happily baptized her. Still, the accusation left a scar that Aunt Iva never forgot.

~

People in the Ozarks are not alone in prizing vignettes. Nearly everyone especially likes to hear or read short stories that are laced with an unexpected and droll sense of humor. A master of this genre was one of my great-uncles, Jeremiah Benjamin Rader, for whom I may have been named. As diminutive as his wife was large, it was said that "Jerry" found his own stories so funny that he too often interrupted them by falling into fits of uncontrollable laughter. One such fit cost him dearly; in 1940, a pork chop that he was eating for supper lodged in his windpipe, choking him to death.

While Ozarkers expected entertainment in their short stories, they also valued them, though perhaps unconsciously, as a means of bringing greater order and clarity to their otherwise indecipherable experiences. If not by storytelling, how else could they explain the tragedies and the triumphs that so often seemed to defy common sense? Jeremiah Benjamin and other Ozarker storytellers preferred vignettes that elevated the importance of individual decision-making at the expense of social or economic forces beyond their control. Stories could thereby strengthen their resolve to act in the face of the most adverse of circumstances. Perhaps equally important, telling such stories helped to make a case for the family's existence as a historic entity. For those families without great fortunes or reputations otherwise, this could be no small feat.

In addition to serving the day-to-day needs of Ozarkers, these vignettes can be considered as primary sources. They potentially offer insights into an American region and, more specifically, American family life. We may imagine them as a set of exploratory postholes. As with those employed at archaeological sites, when unearthed, these core samples may reveal vivid, if incomplete, details of a culture that otherwise remains obscured. Consider the specificity of a few vignettes from this book. Apart from Grandpa delivering babies, readers will come face-to-face with an Ozarks mother (mine) who attributed importance to her first child (me) having been born in a veil, find out why Pap shot Old Polly, and learn how a young woman from the suburbs of Washington, D.C., discovered the oddities of Ozarks banking.

These vignettes frequently challenge notions that the Ozarks are a homogeneous, starkly distinctive region. In some instances, they even reveal qualities of Ozarks life that are characteristic of rural societies everywhere. Consider, for example, a study by an anthropologist of the uses of nicknaming in the 1950s by farmers and villagers in a remote part of Spain. The rural people there echoed almost exactly the way that Ozarkers employed nicknames in my youth.[1] Perhaps it is little wonder that I, as a product of the rural Ozarks, have frequently sensed a stronger affinity with farming people (no matter where they came from) than I have with their urban counterparts.

Its remoteness conceded, the portrait of the Ozarks revealed here is of a region that has been historically less isolated and self-sufficient than is commonly supposed. In particular, the coming of the railroad propelled the region into modernity, which meant not only more rapid and cheaper transportation but also a revolution in communications, the introduction of commercial entertainment, and the arrival of a vast cornucopia of alluring consumer goods depicted in the annual Sears and Roebuck catalogs. True, the Great Depression of the 1930s set back this pell-mell lurch into modernity, but beginning with World War II, it resumed unabated. Indeed, in the postwar period in much of the Ozarks, rural one-room schools, churches, and country stores closed their doors and daily life reoriented itself from the countryside to the nearby small towns and sometimes to larger cities.

These vignettes suggest that not all Ozarks families were or are the same. Far from it! Here, you will find within the rural Shannon County of my early youth at least two distinctive family cultures: the "branch water," that of my mother, and the "creek bottom," that of my father. But these stories indicate that even this division is too simple. Although both of my paternal grandparents were from creek-bottom families, my grandmother's family, that of the Pummills, resembled to a striking degree those attributed to the New England Puritans. The Pummills valued education, hard work, and strong community ties whereas my grandfather's family, the Raders, were far more relaxed. While laboring intensely in planting and harvesting seasons, they prized nothing so much as hunting and fishing.

Neither are the histories and cultures of the counties and neighborhoods within the Ozarks identical. To be sure, there are similarities; above all else, the two neighborhoods in which I came of age shared staggering rates of poverty. But perhaps partly because of its rugged terrain, the Mahans Creek, or Delaware, neighborhood of my early youth was more self-contained. Having in its heyday two churches, a post office, a country store, and several long-established families, it featured stronger social ties than the Schneider neighborhood in which I later lived. But perhaps partly because of its flatter terrain, Howell County, Schneider's home, was in the end far more prosperous than Shannon County, home of the Delaware neighborhood.

Apart from place, these vignettes spring from a particular time, about 1935, the year of my birth, to about 1958, when I left the Ozarks to enter graduate school. They are thus deeply tinged by my personal experience, which included living on farms, farming itself, and attending one-room schools and high school in West Plains, Missouri. After high school graduation in 1953, my perspective on the Ozarks may have begun to change; for the next two and a half years, I worked as a jig builder for the Boeing Aircraft Company in Wichita, Kansas (a city on the Great Plains) and attended the University of Wichita as a part-time student. In 1958, I returned to the Ozarks to finish a bachelor's degree in history from Southwest Missouri State College (now Missouri State University) in Springfield. Then came graduate school and eventually employment at Oklahoma State University, the University of Montana, and the University of Nebraska–Lincoln. No less significant in reshaping my perspective on the Ozarks was my marriage in 1961 to Barbara Koch of Riverdale, Maryland, by whom I subsequently had two children.

When considering the truth of these vignettes, I beg readers to cut me a little slack. They arise mainly from my memory (always fallible) and the memory of others (especially family members). I am also conscious that I have on occasion doubtlessly succumbed to a dictum attributed to another Missourian, Mark Twain: "Never let the truth get in the way of a good story." But even if the details of these episodes fail to always stand up to rigorous scrutiny, I hope that they add up not only to an interesting read, but also to a fuller understanding of an American region.

This book is divided into four parts, each with a separate introduction. The first part revolves around vignettes that are set in an especially rugged place, the Mahans Creek waterway of Shannon County, Missouri, while the second consists of vignettes that are associated with what I call the "goat" farm in the Schneider neighborhood located some six miles outside of West Plains, Missouri. The third part includes glimpses into my family's life on a farm in Gunter's Valley (in the same neighborhood) while the final part presents three reflections on the Ozarks after I went away to college.

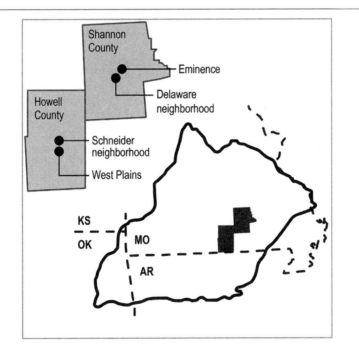

Figure 1. A map of my Ozarks neighborhoods. The neighborhoods of Delaware in Shannon County and Schneider in Howell County, both in southern Missouri, provide the settings for nearly all of the vignettes in this book. Courtesy of Katie Nieland.

ACKNOWLEDGMENTS

My warmest thanks go to the major protagonists in these vignettes. They include kinfolk:

—My parents (now deceased), Lowell "Pap" and Lydia "Mom" (Eddings) Rader, who played major roles in so many of these stories

—My brother Mike, who was not only a cohort in many of my youthful ventures but later abetted my memory of them

—My maternal grandparents (now deceased), Alford "Raz" and Florence Eddings, and my paternal grandfather, Edward Martin "Sam" Rader, as well as my uncle Hulbert Rader (both deceased)

—My sisters Ada Cochran and Alice Smith

—My daughter Anne Rader and son-in-law Ken Gatter

—My first cousins Gloria Dene (Rader) Fry and Jayne Rader

—My second cousin, Arch Pummill (deceased)

—And, of course, the love of my life, Barbara (Koch) Rader, as both a protagonist and an adviser

Thanks for permission to reprint slightly revised versions of two of these vignettes, "The People Living There Even Drank Rainwater from Cisterns" and "Born in a Veil," in *Elder Mountain: A Journal of Ozarks Studies* 10 (2020): 248–51, edited by Philip Howerton and "I Would Choose to Live in Town or Beside a Country Road," *Ozarks Watch: The Magazine of the Ozarks*, 2nd ser., 9, no. 2 (Fall/Winter 2020): 52–53, edited by Susan Croce Kelly.

Others made important contributions both directly and indirectly to the writing of this book. They include Megan Brown, Leigh Ann Cowan, Jill Hickman, Katie Nieland, and Allison Rader. And thanks to Jill and Terrel Hanshew, who repeatedly aided Barbara and me in making life worthwhile through the great coronavirus pandemic of 2019–22. I thank Vanessa Gorman for not only continuing to offer her friendship but also for serving as my computer guru and as my co-teacher of University of Nebraska–Lincoln OLLI (adult seniors learning) courses. Two anonymous reviewers of this manuscript offered useful ideas for revision, some but not all of which I incorporated into the final version. And last but not the least, I acknowledge Alison Syring Bassford, my editor at the University of Illinois Press. At virtually every step in the creation of this book, Alison sustained me with her good cheer and her perceptive responses to what I had written.

When Grandpa Delivered Babies
and Other Ozarks Vignettes

PART I

The Clear, Cold Water
of Mahans Creek

When I was an undergraduate at Southwest Missouri State College in Springfield in the 1950s, I joined a group of Shannon County boys in forming an intramural basketball team. We named our quintet the Ridge Runners. Apart from the reference to the rough terrain from which we came, I would like to think that we chose this name to incite fear into the hearts of opposing teams. Maybe our foes would conclude that we were as adept on the campus hardwoods as the Ozarks bootleggers (also called Ridge Runners) were in the 1920s when they eluded the authorities by skillfully negotiating Shannon County's steep ridges so that they could deliver moonshine to their customers. Given that many Ozarkers were teetotalers, perhaps we also adopted this name as a token form of adolescent rebellion.

Be that as it may, we thought of our unusually rugged habitat as a special place. The dense forests, the caves, the hollows, the steep hills, and above all else, the cold, clear-water creeks and rivers set it apart. Although picturesque enough to conjure up images of a wilderness Arcadia that even the ancient Greeks might have envied, this terrain was not ideal for farming. The streams sliced up the small patches of bottomland into even smaller patches, the topsoil was thin, and rainwater seeped through it quickly. And it was physically isolated. With admirable brevity, the dean of Ozarks studies, Brooks Blevins, once declared that the Mahans Creek neighborhood where I spent the first nine years of my life was (and is) "one of the most remote places in a region renowned for its remoteness."[1]

My paternal ancestors loved this remoteness. It was so much like the countryside that they had left behind. When in 1880 my widowed great-grandmother Nancy Jane Childress Rader first arrived by buckboard wagon at the juncture of Open Hollow and Mahans Creek, the vista surely reminded her of her ancestral homeland in the hills and hollows of Hart County,

Figure 2. Granny Nancy Jane Childress Rader, date unknown but perhaps about 1890 when she was fifty-nine years old. "Headstrong," when the family moved from Kentucky to Missouri, she insisted that they bring along a two-hundred-pound stalagmite taken from the Childress Cave so that it could eventually serve as her tombstone. Upon the death of her husband, George Washington Rader, in 1880, Nancy guided the family through the trials of living in the Mahans Creek neighborhood. She passed away in 1912 at the age of eighty-five. Courtesy of the author.

Kentucky. Delighted with their new homeland, she, her three daughters, and her seven sons at once moved into an abandoned log house. But life was not easy there; they struggled, especially at first, simply to survive. All of Nancy's children except her youngest, Edward "Sam" (who was to become my grandfather), quickly left home to seek their fortunes elsewhere.

"Some went up the holler, some went down the holler, and some went catawampus," explained my uncle Hulbert Rader many years later. Five of the children stayed in the neighborhood, eventually married, and had numerous children of their own. By 1910, their numbers had ballooned to seventy-one, making them the largest family network in Delaware Township. By then, one out of every three residents in the township was related to "Granny" Nancy Jane.

Most of Granny's neighbors had similar origins. After having lived for a time in the eighteenth century in Virginia or the Carolinas, they then had crossed over the mountains into Tennessee and Kentucky. Geographer Terry Jordan-Bychkov has argued that it was here, especially in Tennessee, that a blending of peoples within the cauldron of a unique physical habitat produced an important new American folk region, the Upland South. He summed up some of the region's salient characteristics: a preference for living in wooded "hollers," the development of "a unique nasal dialect," the adoption of a set of special building ways (specifically the log house), a love of "mournful" country music, and a propensity for "clan-based feuding." (Jordan-Bychkov should have added another basic characteristic: a love of hunting and fishing by the menfolk.) From this "hearth" in Tennessee and Kentucky, Jordan-Bychkov wrote, its descendants took their Upland South folkways with them westward into the Ozarks and in due time into Oklahoma and Texas and even into Southern California.[2]

Although there is much to be said in favor of Jordan-Bychkov's analysis of region-making, it is not the whole story—at least not for Shannon County. Early in the county's history, the local residents began to make an important social distinction. They referred to some of their neighbors as the "poo' people," "white trash," or as the "branch-water folk." Many of them lived on the numerous seasonal branches that led up and away from Mahans Creek. Known not only for their poverty, the branch-water folk also suffered from a negative reputation—one by no means totally deserved—for orneriness, which included male lawlessness, moonshining, a propensity for violence, and a negligence of family obligations.

On the other side of the creek's social divide were the more prosperous and respectable, those known as the "creek bottom" families. Fewer in numbers than their branch-water counterparts, they owned more acreage suitable for row cropping and grazing. Their better lands soon enabled a few of them to climb up the neighborhood's social ladder. It was they, and they alone, who had the wherewithal to send their children regularly to the local one-room schools, to build houses of sawed lumber, and to buy the latest consumer goods from the Sears and Roebuck catalogs or from local merchants. During the neighborhood's great timber harvest between about 1892 and 1914, their children began attending the local high schools at Eminence, Winona, or Birch Tree, and more surprisingly, between 1905 and 1915 no fewer than eight young men and women from the neighborhood went away to college. One of them even obtained a PhD degree (my great-uncle Lawrence Pummill) and two of them master's degrees.

We need to take special note of one of the creek-bottom families, that of the Pummills. Headed by John Hezekiah Pummill and his wife, Lydia (Matthews), they stood apart from the other local families. Shockingly for his time and place, John Pummill rejected evangelical Protestantism; he labeled himself a "Unitarian" and insisted that upon death all humans would go to heaven. Equally unusual, only one of the five men in John's immediate family used tobacco!

While the Matthewses' migratory trail across America resembled other families in the creek neighborhood, their family tree was replete with preachers and teachers. Rather than to the central Ozarks during the nineteenth century, Lydia's immediate ancestors had settled on the northern edge of the region, in the Mint Hill neighborhood of Osage County, Missouri, where there were German and French settlers and almost as many Catholics as Protestants. They soon achieved some local prominence. One of her brothers became a local Primitive Baptist preacher (as was her father), a second taught in one-room schools for twenty-three years (including a brief tenure teaching Black children during Reconstruction), voters elected a third to serve as a county court judge, and a fourth became a successful farmer and veterinarian.

At least two brothers were active Masons and all of them were said to be "Republicans with a capital *R*." The Raders of the day, on the other hand, were Democrats, though I am not sure it should be said with a capital *D*, for they might be more appropriately called Jacksonian Democrats. Even in the days of Franklin D. Roosevelt, they began to drift away from the party of their ancestors and with the civil rights movement and the cultural upheaval of the 1960s, in the late twentieth and early twenty-first centuries, a majority of them became Republicans.

John Pummill's ancestors followed a different migratory trail. They traced their family tree back to the seventeenth century, to the tiny village of Sidestrand, England, a hotbed of Puritanism. It is possible, indeed perhaps likely, that his predecessors passed remnants of Puritan piety down from one generation to the next. What is even more important is the Pummill family's history in America. Their migration took them across the periphery (in southern Ohio and central Missouri) rather than the heartland of the Upland South. True, as with their neighbors, the Pummill menfolk loved to hunt and to fish, but influenced more than the Raders by the ways of the Upper Midwest, they also esteemed learning, hard work, and civic engagement. If the issue were one of trading two dogs for two pigs, my uncle Gilbert Rader once quipped, the Raders would opt to keep the dogs while the Pummills would choose the pigs!

The first vignette recounts the background, courtship, and marriage of my parents, Lowell Rader and Lydia Eddings, in Shannon County, Missouri.

1

"You'd Better Treat Her Right"

Since his natural father had died six months before he was born (in 1884), Alford "Raz" Eddings, my maternal grandfather who was to become a neighborhood "midwife," began life with a handicap. His situation worsened when he was thirteen. A quarrel, the subject of which is unknown, erupted between him and his new stepfather, who consequently banned him from the family's household. Thereafter, Raz lived with various kinfolk before venturing out on his own as a timber worker in Shannon County, Missouri. In 1910, Raz finally settled down when, as a twenty-six-year-old, he married a fifteen-year-old local girl, Madie Florence George. The couple borrowed enough money to buy a mostly hillside 160-acre farm up in McHenry Hollow.

Like many branch-water families of the day, the couple's main claim to success was in having children, lots of them, eventually one boy and ten surviving girls. On at least one occasion, Florence made it plain that she was none too happy about this accomplishment. One of her daughters, Iva, found her crying behind the house. "What's the matter, Ma?" asked Iva. "I'm pregnant again. I can't keep him off of me," Florence responded.[3] Neither is it likely that Raz was altogether pleased with this situation. As

Figure 3. The home of the Raz and Florence Eddings family as it looked in 2016. Raz himself built this single-walled "sawmill" house in about 1920. It consisted of a kitchen/storage area, a bedroom for Raz and Florence, a small bedroom for their only son, Alford, and a larger bedroom for the ten daughters who slept in bunk beds. While the Eddings family left there in 1935, it continued to be occupied by other families until the end of the twentieth century. Courtesy of the author.

a farmer, he could have used more strong-armed sons and fewer daughters. His only son—also named Alford—did not turn out well. Young Alford would go into the town of Eminence on Saturdays and regularly drink to excess. To sleep off his drunken sprees, Sheriff Bum Powell did the family a favor by routinely locking him up overnight in the county jail.

On the other hand, one of his daughters, the oldest one, Lydia (my mother), was a gem; nobody could ask for a better daughter. From early childhood, Lydia took on an oversized role within the family. She not only behaved well, but she also aided Florence with household chores and in rearing the younger girls. She even helped Raz by bringing in the cows, milking them, and doing other farm chores. In the spring of 1933, at the age of seventeen, she became the first and only member of the Eddings family to graduate from high school. She dreamed of becoming a one-room rural schoolteacher, but the times were bad. It was in the midst of the Great Depression, so there was a surfeit of qualified teachers in Shannon County. The next year, 1934, fate intervened in her life again when twenty-seven-year-old Lowell Rader came a-courting.

What the Eddings family knew about Lydia's suitor is open to conjecture. Kinfolk in Eminence may have told them that Lowell's father, Sam, owned a good farm down on Mahans Creek and that he was thus a member of a creek-bottom family. They could have even learned that Lowell's deceased (1913) mother, Ada May, was from the more distinguished Pummill family. Perhaps they also knew that one of Ada and Sam's daughters had married into the Rhinehart family, who owned a big spread in Spring Valley up near where the Eddings family lived. They may have been the most renowned family in Shannon County.

What they didn't know about Lowell was probably more substantial. His shyness as a youngster had nearly paralyzed him. He was so afraid of attending school that Sam had permitted him to remain home until he was eight years old. Although Lowell struggled in the classroom, he eventually finished grade school and, as student at Eminence high school, exhibited flashes of excellence on the basketball floor at the Opera House. But after his freshman year, he dropped out of school, the only one of Sam and Ada Rader's seven children not to finish high school. He at once settled back onto the family farm, toiling with Sam and his two younger brothers and occasionally working as a hand on the Rhinehart ranch. His future was far from promising.

Lowell's life took an unexpected turn in 1926. That year, his older brother Gilbert, who had been convalescing from tuberculosis and working in Arizona, and his new bride, Dene, returned to Shannon County for a visit to the family farm. Details of the visit have been lost, but it seems safe in retrospect to guess that the young couple regaled the wide-eyed family with the wonders of Prescott, Arizona. Above all else, there were jobs there. Indeed, Gib may have assured Lowell that he could get him an apprenticeship as an electrician in the same shop, the Vyne Brothers Electric Company, in which he worked.

Lowell took the plunge; he left the familiar confines of the Ozarks and at once found employment with the Vyne Brothers. It was in Prescott that he seems to have begun to reinvent himself. In this mile-high, wide-open mining town of some five thousand residents, he encountered strange people—Native Americans, immigrants from southern and eastern Europe, Chinese Americans, and Mexican Americans. Catholics probably outnumbered Protestants and men outnumbered women. Despite national prohibition, whiskey flowed freely in the downtown saloons. Upstairs, "ladies of the evening" offered their wares. Although Lowell likely resisted these allures—at least most of them—he seems to have experienced a transfusion of confidence. He began dating a young Mexican American woman, Rose Contreras. They married in 1928.

The marriage did not last. In 1930, the Rader brothers, along with their spouses and Gilbert's two children, decided to return to Mahans Creek where they jointly took up farming on the old Pummill place. Even though there were few if any Roman Catholics in Shannon County (let alone Mexican Americans), Rose at first seemed to fit into her new circumstances well. Nobody, it seems, thought that she was dissatisfied with Lowell or with living on an isolated farm in the Ozarks. Rose birthed a son on Christmas Eve 1931 who died from "acute bronchitis" thirteen days later. Maybe she fell into a postpartum depression. In any case, in December 1932, Rose took the train back to Prescott, Arizona, allegedly to visit her family. She never returned. In August 1933, Lowell successfully sued her for divorce on the grounds of desertion.

Characteristically of Ozarkers of that day, Lowell's female kinfolk quickly proposed candidates for Rose's replacement, among them Lydia Eddings.[4] Introduced to the comely lass up in McHenry Hollow by his sister-in-law, Lowell wasted no time. Approaching the Eddings farm in a shay pulled by a white horse, his voice echoed up and down the holler as he yodeled "My Lydia," a song he had written for his new sweetheart. He cut a dashing figure, indeed, Lydia's younger sisters remembered.

He apparently proposed on their first date, but Raz had something to say about this sudden turn of events. After all, Lydia's suitor was nine years older than she was and, more importantly, a divorced man. Raz sat Lowell down and, according to family lore, said to him, "You'd better treat her right, 'cause she always has a home to come to here." As noble as Raz's words were, they may have rung a bit hollow, for the Eddings family was in dire financial straits. Already, they had agreed to turn their farm over to creditors. In 1935, they sold most of their belongings at a public auction and abandoned the Ozarks. They went into sharecropping on the wheat farm of a distant cousin outside of Wellington, Kansas.

In the meantime, Lydia and Lowell in effect merged branch- and creek-bottom families with their marriage on May 30, 1934. The next year, they moved into a log house on an eighty-acre farm that they had bought on Mahans Creek, and on August 25, 1935, I was born.

The vignettes that follow begin with my birth and continue with my life as a child on Mahans Creek from 1935 to my immediate family's departure from Shannon County in 1944.

2

I Was Born in a Veil

My mother, Lydia, believed in omens. She was not alone. Just about everybody secretly does. If pressed, they are likely to feel uneasy about a black cat crossing their path or rain falling on their wedding day. There are also good omens such as meeting a cow on a country road or having a bird doo-dooing on your head.

That Mom was especially receptive to signs arose partly from her upbringing. She had been born in an extraordinarily secluded place, McHenry Holler. No neighbor's house or farm was within sight. And the unpredictable forces of nature were ever present. As with many rural folk of that day, the Eddings family employed "signs," including especially unusual natural phenomenon such as a cloudburst or the birth of a deformed baby, to understand the world around them. No responsible family dug a well without first using a divining rod (a forked limb) to locate underground water or castrated a pig without first consulting the phases of the moon.

Having grown up in this world of signs and spirits, you can only imagine the importance my mom attributed to my birth. For I was not only her firstborn, but I was also born with a veil—a thin birth membrane covering my face. Such is a rare phenomenon indeed, only about one in every eighty thousand births.[5] Cultures extending at least as far back as the ancient Greeks and Romans have attributed to such children great wisdom, foresight, and luck. At birth, according to legend, Jesus Christ himself had a hood or caul over his face. So did Sigmund Freud. Not only this, but such babies were reputedly far easier to rear than their less fortunate counterparts.

Almost at once, doubts about the age-old prophecies surrounding born-in-a-veil babies must have arisen in my mother's mind. For I was *not* a tranquil baby with a smiling disposition. Far from it! Rather than welcoming entry into the world of the Great Depression of the 1930s, I yearned for the comfort of the womb. The log cabin in which we lived had no air-conditioning, no electricity, no running water, and no indoor toilet. The heat that summer and the following one broke all local records. Sleeping haphazardly and given to colic, I made life miserable for both of my parents.

Still, somehow Mom survived my trying infancy and continued to look for portends that I was something special. I had a competitor, one who made invidious comparisons possible: a cousin, Catherine "Kitty" Pummill, my age, who lived on the other side of the ridge separating our two farms. As a preschooler, Kitty—effortlessly it seemed—memorized dozens of nursery rhymes, her numbers, and I think, even the alphabet. Maybe she could read a little as well.

My mom, perhaps reluctantly, joined in the competition. After all, her baby had been born in a veil. But it was a mistake. Even though she drilled me relentlessly, I exhibited virtually no aptitude for mastering the subjects that came so easily for my cousin. On one occasion, I think I remember that we both broke down in tears. Or maybe it was just me.

I am guessing at this point in her life that Mom must have lost virtually all faith in the baby-born-in-a-caul omen. It was not easy, however, for her to banish it completely. Throughout her later life, she would continue at least jokingly to say that she expected great things from me.

Figure 4. Lowell (Pap), Lydia (Mom), and (left to right) my brother Mike and I. Photo taken I think at Alley Spring, Missouri in about 1940, when I was five years old. Courtesy of the author.

3

Learning the Hard Way

Maybe I was no match for Kitty Pummill when it came to formal learn-ing. But I think that I could hold my own, or even spurted ahead of her, when it came to the acquisition of knowledge about other important mat-ters that arose from living on Ozarks farms. On our Mahans Creek farm as well as our farms in Howell County, I learned about the "facts of life" the hard way—that is, via direct experience. Specifically, this meant watching Pap try to break a horse to harness, the breeding of farm animals, the birth-ing of their offspring, and "putting them down" when they were no longer useful.

A few examples.

When I was about four-years old, Pap bought an "unbroken" filly from a neighbor for a bargain price. Although this neighbor had failed to bring the young mare to heel as a work horse, Pap, perhaps because of previous experience, was confident that he could "break" her. And he had no inten-tion of spending a lot of time at the task; as usual, he was in a hurry. To him, slowly prepping the horse for harness by gradually gaining her trust was a waste of time. Setting out to crush her wild spirit at once, he harnessed her in tandem to our farm wagon with an older, presumably well-trained horse. He then hopped into the wagon, took the reins in hand, slapped the animals across their rumps, and yelled, "Gidda-up!"

In a bid to escape confinement, the wild-eyed filly lunged pell-mell out of the barn and into the open field. Frightened by the behavior of her mate, the older horse also broke into a gallop. Standing up in the wagon with his legs planted apart for balance, Pap tried to slow the team by pulling back on their reins as best he could and yelling, "Whoa!" to no avail. Despite the steel bits biting painfully into their mouths, around and around the field the two horses ran at full tilt. Their mouths frothing, both animals as well as Pap broke into rivulets of sweat. The reins became so slick that Pap could not hold on to them; he finally resorted to putting them into his mouth and clamping down on them with his teeth. Still, he could not bring the runaway horses to a halt. After what seemed like an interminable time for me, the young mare finally stumbled and fell to the ground, exhausted. White lather covered her body.

At first, Pap thought he had won the battle of wills. But he soon discovered instead that he had "broken the wind" of the untamed horse. For the uninitiated, this meant that the filly's respiratory system had been permanently damaged. Even if broken to harness, she could no longer process enough oxygen to do heavy-duty farmwork. Pap faced a painful decision. Instead of killing her as a worthless farm animal as some farmers would have done, he turned her out onto the "open range" of the nearby woods to fend for herself.

I am unsure whether Pap thought she could survive on her own or not. But in any case, several years later, upon visiting the farm after we had moved to Howell County, Missouri, I looked across the fence separating our Shannon County farm from the woods, and there stood the mare, older and perhaps wiser but apparently wistfully somehow seeking to reconnect to the farm. The scene was so poignant that I have never forgotten it.

Something else on the farm that I have never forgotten: the frenzied behavior of cows when they are "in heat." (In heat is a euphemism for the phase in the estrus cycle in which the animal, if not pregnant, is amenable to being bred by a bull or artificially inseminated.) Suddenly, when in heat, a normally placid cow behaves in shocking ways. Loud, mournful bellows by the cow might awaken a sleepy farm family before dawn; they might then even observe the cows sniffing one another's genitalia and the cow in heat standing still while being mounted by the other cows or by a bull. I am unsure when I learned that adult human females did not behave similarly, but as a youngster, I am guessing that it may have caused me some confusion.

Neither are memories of the birth of farm animals easily forgotten. The most vivid of these occurred when I was about twelve years old. Arriving home from school, I observed one of our young ewes giving birth in a nearby field. Upon further investigation, I saw that part of the lamb's legs were extending out the ewe's birth canal and I soon sensed that she was in distress. Whether I had seen Pap help deliver a lamb or a calf, I am unsure, but in any case, I decided to assist the young ewe. I grasped the slick legs of the lamb and, with more effort than I expected to exert, extracted it slowly from its mother's uterus. I was then delighted to see the young ewe turn around and begin licking the wet afterbirth off her newborn. The lamb, though wobbly, soon stood up and began to nurse.

As often as not, the facts of farm life ended less happily than in this instance. For example, the local dairy farmers in Howell County typically faced a conundrum when it came to breeding their milk cows. On the one hand, the farmer could breed the cow (usually a Jersey) to a Jersey bull and thereby hope that the offspring would be a female that could eventually be added to the family's dairy herd. But alas, chances were equal that the calf might be male for which the farmer was less likely to want to keep; usually, the males were destined for a quick exit to the slaughterhouse.

Another option promised the possibility of more earnings. The farmer might breed his milk cow to a bigger beef bull such as an Angus or a Hereford and thereby produce a much larger calf for eventual slaughter. Such "crossbreeding," though a common practice, had its perils, for the ensuing calf might be so big that its small mother would die while trying to deliver it.

Culling farm animals represented yet another brutish side of living on the farm. Calculating farmers knew that to maximize their incomes, they had to foreshorten the life of their animals. In the case of chickens, this meant killing and eating nearly all the males while young and tender. If females, it meant that when the hen aged and failed to lay her quota of eggs, she was destined for the Sunday stewpot.

Likewise, clever farmers typically culled (sold or ate) the least productive of their cows or hogs. Although a typical sow could produce two healthy litters a year, few of them could be bred after four or five years of age. After that, off to the local slaughterhouse or into the family's smokehouse they usually went. Upon finding that his four- or five-year-old dairy cow could no longer calve and produce milk, calculating farmers also wasted no time in selling them for their meat. I guess that on occasion, sentiment overrode practicality because I recall that Pap allowed at least one cow that he especially treasured to hang around the farm until she died of old age.

I think that most farmers held a somewhat different view of horses than they did of chickens, hogs, or cattle. There were of course those who would sell their aging horses to local butchers who would then render them into meat for dogs and cats, but as you likely know from western movies, a special symbiosis frequently existed between men and their horses. Indeed, in the rural parts of the Upland South in earlier times, a boy was not a man until he had his own horse. When of age in the 1880s, every one of my six male great-uncles on the Rader side of the family acquired or was given his own horse. Likewise, unless they became quite ill or arthritic, I believe that Pap allowed his hounds to die from old age.

Notice in the following vignette the presence of the past, especially of Mahans Creek's golden age, in my early childhood.

4

The Artifacts of Shannon County's Golden Age

When moseying about on our Mahans Creek farm between 1935 and 1944, my younger brother Mike and I routinely came across the artifacts of earlier inhabitants. The log house in which we lived had itself once belonged to a Mahan, the name of the family from which the neighborhood obtained its name. It consisted of two rooms—a living room/bedroom/all-purpose room and a kitchen/storage area. Scattered on the fields of our farm, we also encountered the former presence of the first Americans: arrowheads apparently left behind by Osage hunters.

Haunting reminders of the Native peoples arose from local place names as well. There was the Delaware School itself, named for a band of Indians who had farmed at least one summer near the mouth of Mahans Creek. So enamored were the children at my one-room school with this bit of historical trivia that they on occasion named their athletic teams "Indians." By describing themselves as "hostile" and "bloodthirsty savages," the students even contributed to the prevailing stereotypes of Native Americans. Finally, there was a local legend that the Cortereva one-room school over on the Current River obtained its name from a local Indian chief who had saved a group of Euro-American settlers from a massacre.

Arrowheads were not our only discovery. We found on our farm abandoned steel railway spikes, pieces of decaying rails, and even the remnants of a railroad bridge that had once spanned Mahans Creek. Given our circumstances in the late 1930s and early 1940s, it took a staggering feat of the imagination for us youngsters to conjure up the meaning of these finds. Without a neighbor's house or barn visible in any direction and without even a county-maintained dirt road along the creek, how was it possible that in earlier times bellowing locomotives had crossed our farm heavily laden with thousands of feet of short-leaf pine lumber? Later, we learned that early in the twentieth century, the giant Missouri Lumber and Mining Company had harvested the yellow pine from Shannon County's steep hillsides, sawed and loaded it at their huge sawmill in nearby West Eminence, and then transported it to Winona Crossing and from there to the nation's fast-growing cities.

This was not all. In those days, a passenger train consisting of only one car twice daily made the same trip up and down the creek as the lumber

Figure 5. A log train making its way to the great sawmill located on Mahans Creek in West Eminence, Missouri in the early twentieth century. Courtesy of the author.

trains. One could close one's eyes and imagine Oscar Mahan, the former owner of our farm, flagging down the passenger train so that he could get to the county courthouse in Eminence and pay his taxes on time. My great-uncle Elva Pummill, who twice ran unsuccessfully for public office in Shannon County as a Socialist, even purchased his own handcar to get back and forth to work at the hub mill in West Eminence. Upon hearing the approach of a train, he had to wrestle the heavy handcar off and onto the tracks.

There were yet other reminders of the creek's golden age. Up the creek only about a half mile in the deep woods stood the abandoned Crescent (Buckhart) schoolhouse, which at one time had been crowded with children but had been closed before I started school in 1941. When I visited the headwaters of the creek in 2014 with my cousin Jerome, the building somehow still stood, though part of the floor had given way. Jerome and I also examined the remains of several nearby houses once occupied by timber workers or "branch water" farmers. When I was a child, only one family of three adults still lived in this part of the Mahans Creek watershed. No one lived there in 2014. Down the creek, still visible to this day, are the hulking remains of the great sawmill at West Eminence.

By the time Mike and I appeared on the creek in the mid-1930s, a lot had changed. It had been at least two decades since the timber industry or the railroad had pumped thousands of dollars into the local economy. No longer did all but a few of the families in the creek watershed have the financial wherewithal to buy lace curtains, pianos, or Victrolas. No longer did the neighborhood's civic and social life enjoy the same vitality that it had had in the golden age. No longer could you watch a silent movie on the weekend at the Delaware schoolhouse or watch a balloon ascend over the schoolhouse. Still, as you will read in the introduction to part 2, despite or perhaps because of the Great Depression, the neighborhood did experience something of a renewal in the 1930s only to see associational life weakened yet again when America entered World War II in 1941.

In other respects, the Great Depression pressed on its residents a retreat into the past. To cope with the exigencies of the difficult times, the families tried to "make do." They became more self-sufficient. They grew more of their own foodstuffs. As never before, they canned record-setting gallons of fruits and vegetables. It was said, doubtless with exaggeration, that during the Great Depression my immediate family survived by eating the watercress that grew in the creek. Without the means to buy store-bought items, I remember my mother making foul-smelling soap from pig fat and the lye from ashes. She transformed flour sacks into shirts and smocks. She washed clothes in a huge tub and rinsed them out by running them through a hand-cranked wringer.

No Moses ever returned to Shannon County to deliver its peoples back into the Promised Land of the early twentieth century. Even today, there is not a single stoplight, a single chain motel or hotel, a single railroad, and only one fast-food restaurant (a Subway in a Winona gas station) in the entire county. Only the artifacts remain as visible reminders of the county's golden age.

5

Every Child Needs a Grandpa

As I walked across the Southwest Missouri State College gymnasium to the History Department desk where I intended to enroll for classes in 1957, a wiry man in his sixties rushed across the floor toward me. It was my great-uncle Lawrence Pummill, the head of the college's mathematics department. I was somewhat surprised that he even recognized me since I had not seen him for some time.

He at once launched into a discussion with the history adviser, Duane Meyer, a junior faculty member who several years later would become president of the college. I do not remember his exact words, but he told Meyer that I was his nephew and, I think, commended me as a prospective student. In any case, I have always thought that this introduction to the college served me well. Even though I hardly knew Uncle Lawrence in a personal sense, I owed him a memorable debt.

Recently, this got me thinking about the roles of adults (in particular kinfolk) in the lives of children. Every child needs adults other than their parents to ease their thorny path toward maturity. Today, I think, there are fewer of these adults than in the past. My wife, Barbara, a piano teacher, has observed that piano lessons are one of the few situations in which children today have a one-to-one relationship with an adult other than their parents. Fortunately for me while a child on Mahans Creek, I had such an adult in my life, my grandfather Sam Rader.

The youngest of eleven children, Grandpa had been born on a farm in 1874 in Hart County, Kentucky. Typical of many upland southern boys,

Figure 6. Aunt Elsie Rhinehart, Sam's oldest daughter, and Grandpa Sam Rader in the 1930s. Courtesy of the author.

his rearing was indulgent and permissive but in his instance, unusually so. Without his father who had died from a logging accident when he was only six years old, Sam's mother and his older siblings doted on him. Unlike many in his neighborhood, he liked school and he gained something of a local reputation for his skills at playing the fiddle at square dances and singing old Kentucky folk ballads. In 1896, he married Ada Pummill. They had seven children before her death in 1913. He always said that his children, who upon Ada's death ranged from sixteen years to fourteen months old, reared themselves. Still, few parents exerted more influence on their children than Sam. Every one of them exhibited their love for him throughout his life.

Maybe we (his grandchildren as well as his own seven children) liked him so much because he always seemed so preternaturally young. I remember as a child that Grandpa, who was in his late sixties, astonished Pap with his physical agility and strength while aiding him in fixing a washed-out water gate in the creek. His own children called him Sam rather than Dad or Pa. "In many ways, he was one of us boys," recalled Hub, one of his four sons, "especially w[h]en it came to hunting, fishing, swimming and eating watermelon."[6] When plowing corn or putting up hay in July or August, Hub remembered, Sam might call a halt to the sweltering labor and join his sons by stripping off his clothes and jumping into the ever-so-cold creek. His granddaughter Gloria Dene fondly remembered him in the 1930s making her a miniature farm from cornstalks and corncobs.

No memory of mine is more vivid than the Sunday afternoon watermelon feeds that Grandpa hosted. A dozen or so kinfolk and neighbors gathered in his yard under a canopy of immense oak trees. From his well, Grandpa retrieved several huge, cold watermelons that he had grown in the sandy soil near the creek. We sliced the melons into eighths and then into sixteenths so they could be eaten directly without the aid of forks or knives. The juices from the delectably sweet melons ran down our chins and onto our hands. We spit the seeds out onto the ground. We washed our hands and faces from a dipper of cold water drawn from Grandpa's well. Grandpa's coonhounds joined in the feast. Known far and wide for their love of melons, the dogs ate the discarded rinds. Sometimes Grandpa even slipped them a regular piece of melon. With a twinkle in his eyes, he enjoyed watching them gobble down the exquisitely sweet fruit.

Off and on, we—that is, my mother, my brother Mike, and me—lived with Grandpa in his small bungalow. This was because in response to the Great Depression, Pap was away—in Kansas or Illinois working as an electrician or a roustabout to earn the family much-needed cash. Not only did Grandpa put out the welcome mat to his daughter-in-law and her two children, but also, I suppose Mom preferred living there to managing a household by herself in our small cabin up the creek. As it happened, the US Census of 1940, locally recorded by my uncle Hub, reported Mom, my younger brother Mike, and me as living in Grandpa's house. Pap does not appear anywhere in that census.

Among my fondest memories was listening to the long discussions of Pap and Grandpa. I sat in utter awe as they reminisced about family and neighborhood history or discussed the validity of various religious beliefs and practices.

Not all my recollections are so pleasant. When I was about four years old, I awoke in the wee hours of the morning to shouts of alarm and to the sweet smell of burning horseflesh. Grandpa's barn was afire. Not only did he lose his barn but also, I think, a couple of horses and maybe a few cows. As far as I can recall, Grandpa took this setback in stride. Indeed, I can never remember him saying anything in anger or, unlike many of his neighbors, ever saying anything negative about Blacks, Catholics, or Jews.

On another occasion, Grandpa, Uncle Hub, and perhaps Uncle Merle dammed Mahans Creek in order irrigate a thirsty watermelon patch and a small cornfield. The dam resulted in a small lake or pond. Since I had wallowed or "swam" in the creek since birth, I apparently presumed (as a five-year-old, I think) that I could swim across the pool. But as I neared the middle, whatever swimming skills I had suddenly vanished; I began to bob up and down and to think that I might drown. Within seconds, Grandpa, dressed in heavy work shoes and overalls, jumped into the water and pulled me out. Perhaps he had saved my life!

After my immediate family left Mahans Creek in 1944, we continued to visit kinfolk in that neighborhood, but in time, my relationship with Grandpa became less personal. That changed somewhat in 1950, when he spent a couple of weeks with us on our farm near West Plains, Missouri. A painful memory accompanies that visit. For reasons that I don't remember, while harnessing our team of horses, I was out of sorts on a Saturday morning. As a fifteen-year-old, I was trying out my cursing skills. Just as I was finishing these combined tasks, I turned around, and standing there was Grandpa. He did not say a word. A slight smile crossed his face. I didn't say anything either.

Two weeks later, he was dead, from a heart attack, but still, his quiet legacy lives on. Every child needs at least one such adult in their life.

6

When Uncle Hub Put Down the Great Delaware School Uprising of 1941

I was woefully unprepared for beginning school in 1941, having spent my first six years in our log cabin on an isolated farm on Mahans Creek. I had never attended kindergarten nor, I think, had I ever been to a Sunday school. And as you know, efforts by my mother to prepare me for school by teaching me nursery rhymes, numbers, and letters had for the most part utterly failed.

Perhaps I exaggerate. I did have an immediate playmate, my brother Mike, and I did live in a neighborhood full of kinfolk. On the other side of the steep ridge in Open Holler lived three Pummill cousins and down the creek two Rader cousins, all about my age and with whom I occasionally played. Before I arrived for my first day of school, I must have known at least casually several of the other students since about a third of them were probably kinfolk.

Still, the first day of school for a first grader could be traumatic. Such was the case for my younger brother Mike, who, in the following year, when the teacher showed him to his tiny desk, burst into tears. (By exaggerating the dangers that he was likely to encounter when attending school, it is likely that I contributed to Mike's fears.) For what seemed to me an embarrassingly long time, no one knew what to do. Finally, much to my relief, Donnie Pummill, an older cousin—I think he was in the fifth grade—suggested that

Mike sit with him. An experienced school mom, Miss Drewell (actually, she was Mrs. Drewell who many years earlier had been my father's teacher in the same one-room rural school) agreed to this unorthodox arrangement. At once, Mike stopped crying and after a few days began to sit at his own desk without incident.

~

Back to the previous school year. The one-room school included students ranging in ages from five to sixteen scattered across eight grades. For most purposes, the teacher divided the school into four groups—that is, she combined first and second graders, third and fourth graders, and so on. After the Pledge of Allegiance to the flag and perhaps the students singing a patriotic song or two (it was wartime), the teacher would begin the day by calling the first graders to the front of the room for a "recitation." (In retrospect, it seems somewhat strange to me that we never said the Lord's Prayer or engaged in other kind of religious practice in the eight years that I attended one-room schools.) The teacher would then proceed in a similar matter through the other groups. Much of the curriculum revolved around trying to learn how to read, spell, write in cursive, and do elementary arithmetic.

Keeping order in such a school was no easy task, especially for someone only a couple of years or so older than some of the eighth-grade students. Such was the case with my first teacher, a Miss Eulah Davis. Almost at once, some of the oldest boys began to test the behavioral boundaries that she tried to impose on them. Before long, the miscreants were doing about as they pleased. When we recessed for noonday lunch, they frequently left the schoolgrounds and headed for Mahans Creek, where they would play, perhaps fish a little, and swim, but they frequently did not return to school that afternoon. They also more or less terrorized the younger children. I remember that one of them threw my prized rubber ball under the schoolhouse. Because of my fear of venomous snakes, I did not try to retrieve it.

In time, the whole school degenerated into chaos. I am unsure precisely how this came about but my uncle Hulbert, the president of the school board, decided that the situation was no longer tolerable. (Incidentally, Miss Eulah was Uncle Hub's sister-in-law.) So Uncle Hub, who himself

Figure 7. Miss Eulah Davis, my first-grade teacher in 1941–42. Courtesy of Jayne Rader.

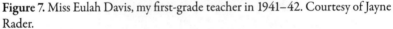

had taught one-room schools as a younger man, called the rebellious older boys into the schoolhouse while Miss Eulah took all of the other children outside. Uncle Hub then ordered each boy to step forward separately, to drop his pants, and to lean over the teacher's desk. Removing his belt, Uncle Hub proceeded to give each of them at least one resounding whack across the butt. (Even though I was outside, I think, but perhaps this is only in my imagination, I remember hearing not only the crack of the belt but also the ensuing cries of pain.) The punishment worked. Uncle Hub had put down the great Delaware School uprising of 1941.

I later learned that Miss Eulah subsequently suffered something of a nervous breakdown. The school board then appointed her sister and Hub's wife, Aunt Wilma, as our new substitute teacher. An experienced teacher, Aunt Wilma was a no-nonsense person. Although previously, as a first grader, I had done pretty much as I pleased (on one occasion using my scissors to trim the hair of a female student who occupied the desk directly in front of me) and learned virtually nothing, I was scared of Aunt Wilma. Out of utter fear, just as did the teenaged boys, I also reformed my behavior . . . well, at least a little.

The following two vignettes treat aspects of child-rearing ways down on Mahans Creek.

7

"Yes, and Alta Won't Like It Either"

In 1938, my cousin Donald "Donny" Pummill, a spirited second grader at Delaware's one-room school, got into trouble with his teacher for repeatedly showing up late for school. "If you are tardy one more time," she warned Donny, "I am going to have to tell your pa."

Donny acknowledged that this was a serious matter, so he added, "Yes, and Alta won't like it either."

"Who is Alta?" asked the teacher.

"Oh, that is Dave's wife," explained Donny.[7]

Friedrich Nietzsche, an influential if demented German thinker, once famously observed that names and naming always involves *power*. If you impose a name on something, it gives you additional control over that something. Esoteric stuff, indeed, but I think you can grasp Nietzsche's insight by acknowledging that Donny (by employing the first names of his parents when responding to his teacher) had placed them on the same level as himself. He had in effect issued a resounding public declaration: "I am the equal to my parents!"

Did the elder Pummills take offense at Donny's assertion of equality? I don't think so. That Dave, Alta, or perhaps even more likely, Donny's grandfather Arthur Pummill reported this student-teacher exchange to the Pummill family's monthly newsletter in 1938 suggests that the adults in his family *approved* of the youngster's forwardness.

Not surprisingly because I think it was commonplace in this era of Ozarks history for parents to encourage among (especially) their male children brazen behaviors that others might consider as unruly and lacking in deference. That Donny was apparently uncowed by the adult authority represented in his teacher and his parents suggested that the boy was on his way to holding his own in an adult world. So instead of condemning his forwardness, I am guessing that the adults in his life were proud of him, or at the least, they found his response amusing.

8

The Preacher's Complaint

Another example of parenting ways in the Ozarks. Curiously, after we had moved to Howell County, Missouri in 1944, my brother Mike and I frequently sat apart from our parents during church services in Schneider's one-room schoolhouse. I never knew why, but I suppose this represented some form of preadolescent or perhaps later on adolescent independence on our part.

At one evening service, perhaps it was more than one, I sat in the very back row and whittled a stick while the preacher held forth about such weighty subjects as heaven and hell. (Whittling was an ancient spare-time activity among Ozarkers.) Afterward, Pap called me aside. He said, "Ben, I don't mind you whittling during the preacher's sermon, but the preacher tells me that it distracts him. So I think you'd better stop."

Although I did discontinue whittling during church services, I had little or no sympathy for the preacher's position. But later when I became a college professor, I came to a better appreciation of the preacher's viewpoint. In classes of one hundred or more students, it was not always the eager faces awaiting learning that caught your attention, but as often as not, it was the lone student or so whom you knew heard nary a word you said.

The following vignette considers the food and eating ways of people in the Ozarks.

9

"Come 'n' Get It"

So announced my grandmother Florence Eddings to everyone within earshot when she had everything ready to eat. Even as a teenager, there was something about her commanding voice and her choice of words that annoyed me. Perhaps it reminded me of taking out a bucket of slop to feed the pigs. As you may know, when pigs recognize that they are about to be fed, a Darwinian scramble ensues. The winners are those pigs who, by bullying their way to the trough, succeed in gobbling up more food faster than their fellow pigs. Hardly a model for human behavior, is it?

Figure 8. Grandpa and Grandma Eddings, about 1950, in Wichita, Kansas. Courtesy of the author.

To be sure, I exaggerate. Eating at Grandma's table fell short of an all-out "root, hog, or die" scramble to consume as much food as quickly as you could. Still, it was an occasion in which the occupants at the table proceeded to eat quickly and without fanfare or ceremony. No one said grace; indeed, rarely did anyone say much of anything. Eating a meal at her table reminded me of filling my car's empty gas tank. There was, however, an inexplicable convention at her house: You could not eat the last portion of a dish. I guess it was understood that the last bite should be reserved for the cook or perhaps to be put into the slop for the family's hounds or their pigs.

I preferred my own mother's way of announcing a meal. In a quiet, considerate voice, she would simply state that breakfast, dinner, or supper was ready to eat. On Sundays or other special times, Pap might even say grace before we began eating. However, no matter how important the occasion, no one ever proposed a toast. No alcohol beverages accompanied our meals. My family were teetotalers. Given that eight or more people of widely disparate ages frequently gathered to eat at the same time, extended discussions of any topics were rare.

If my mother and grandmother represented two variants of Ozarks dining, my aunt Dene Rader exemplified yet a third. Perhaps this was because neither Aunt Dene (even though she had been born in a Nebraska soddy) nor Uncle Gilbert, her husband, were typical Ozarkers. Despite birth and childhood on Mahans Creek and attendance at Delaware's one-room school, Uncle Gilbert was a high school graduate, had even completed some college work, and he belonged to a Masonic order. As a Fleischmann's yeast salesman in northern Arizona during the 1920s, he traveled from one mining camp to another where he allegedly even learned a smattering of Spanish. While there, he met Udene, "Dene," a woman with exquisite tastes and good manners who was employed in her sister's photography studio in Prescott, Arizona. In Prescott, Gilbert and Dene married and had two children, but shortly after the Great Crash in October 1929, the couple moved to the Missouri Ozarks.

At once, they plunged into the local social scene. According to the weekly, the *Current Wave*, on April 25, 1930, they "royally entertained" the junior and senior classes of Eminence High School. To everyone's amazement, they even hired an airplane and a pilot to take those students and guests willing to risk life and limb up for "thrilling rides" over Mahans Creek. Aunt Dene also helped to organize and served as the longtime president of the NTW (Nobility, Truth, and Wisdom), an exclusive literary club of ten or so of Eminence's most prominent housewives. For those envious women not invited to join, according to one source, the acronym more accurately stood for "nasty, talking women." Be that as it may, in time, the couple built a gleaming white, two-story house perched on the hillside overlooking the town. Uncle Gilbert, who had been a basketball star in high school and college, was an all-around athlete. He even laid out a tennis court next to their house. It was, I think, only one of two tennis courts in the entire Shannon County.

Given this context, you can imagine my youthful anxiety about eating there. Unlike the informal and modest circumstances of eating in our log house on Mahans Creek where we ate on benches, Aunt Dene had a formal dining room, a crocheted tablecloth, and a formal setting of dishes, forks, and knives. Never have I been more mortified than, once while eating there, I attempted to slice off a bite-size piece of beef. The meat slid off my plate and onto Aunt Dene's pristine tablecloth. To her credit, she graciously took charge of my disaster, but to this day, I have not forgotten my faux pas.

~

Tradition and circumstances determined the kinds of food that my immediate family on Mahans Creek and even later in Howell County ate. Typical of Ozarkers, at least in the pre-1950 era, we rarely consumed beef in any form. Before the coming of electricity and modern refrigeration to the rural areas, beef was difficult to preserve. Pork and chicken were another matter. A fried chicken, if the chicken was young or if older, stewed, could easily be eaten in one meal. And by salting and curing, pork could remain edible indefinitely. Bacon was popular, a variety of pork that for some reason I distasted, perhaps because my mother sometimes included cold pieces of it along with cold, fried eggs in my sandwiches for school lunch. In season, we of course ate lots of vegetables and fruits as desserts. I especially relished wild blackberry cobblers and cherry pies.

My mother was in charge of the family's garden, and for reasons that remain unclear to me to this day, my brother Mike and I considered doing garden work as somehow unmanly. Hence, Mom had to badger us unrelentingly to get us to plow the garden for her, to spread manure on it, to pull weeds, or do anything connected with this "female" enterprise. (However, here, I must confess, we were less than enthusiastic about doing other kinds of farmwork as well!) Incidentally, Mike and I bridged the gender gap in another way. At Pap's insistence, we dried a lot of dishes.

Trumping all other foods in importance during my childhood were beans and corn bread. Eating corn in some form had long occupied a special place among my ancestors, as I am sure it did in most Ozarks families. My family particularly liked to eat it as a bread, often with butter, molasses, honey, or some kind of jam or jelly spread on it, but I also have fond memories of eating it after I had dunked it in milk.

Boiled pinto beans may have even surpassed the significance of corn bread as a part of our diet. As I remember it, my mother soaked the beans overnight and into the next day before cooking them. Sometimes Mom added ham or other pieces of pork to the beans for flavoring. As far as I can remember, none of my large family ever complained about Mom serving too many beans. Indeed, I am virtually sure that all eight members of the family relished them.

But, alas, upon my marriage to Barbara Koch from the Washington, DC suburbs, I learned to my utter surprise that beans were not universally beloved. Barbara abhorred them! Still, somehow, I survived countless years of rarely eating beans except for occasionally heating them up from a can, ordering beans at a Mexican restaurant, or eating cold pork and beans from a can. By the way, the sweetened pork and beans that you find in a can taste quite different from unsweetened pinto beans; I don't like the sweet kind much.

Once when Barbara needed to visit her parents in suburban Maryland, I was left with the care of our daughter Anne (at the time in high school, I think) and our son Steve (in grade school), I of course hit on a simple, delectable solution to feeding them and me. I would make up a batch of pinto beans!

As I recall, the beans tasted okay, but my children, who were spoiled by eating store-bought pizza, reacted negatively to the dinner that I set before them each night. I am unsure that they ever forgave me for trying to impose my favorite Ozarker food on them. I am delighted to learn, however, that my grandniece Karlee Cochran is keeping Ozarks' food traditions alive. According to her grandmother Ada, Karlee loves nothing more than pinto beans and blackberry cobblers. No bona fide Ozarker can possibly argue with these choices!

As an afterthought, I confess that I broadened my tastes a little in later years, even to the extent of enjoying Italy's Cinque Terre's pesto as well as such exotic items as the Chesapeake Bay's blue crabs. On the other hand, I once upon a time took a pass when I had an opportunity to eat pastissada de caval, Verona, Italy's famed horsemeat stew. Neither am I enamored with the prospect of eating the internal organs of any animals.

10

Family Keepsakes

Maybe Oliver Klepzig, one of my many cousins, chose the patriotic lithographs that graced the interior walls of his modest bungalow on Open Hollow Creek because he was a bachelor, a draft dodger, and the son of German immigrants.

His father, Charles, had been born in Leipzig, Germany. As one of only a few local immigrants, Charles cut a wide swath across Shannon County's history. Allegedly, he introduced both barbed and woven wire fencing to the local farmers. Later, Teddy Roosevelt acknowledged his contributions to the community and to the Republican Party by appointing him as the Winona, Missouri postmaster. Upon his retirement from that position in 1908, the *Current Wave*, a Democratic weekly, generously conceded that although "Uncle Charley" had had the handicap of being a "faithful Republican," he had rendered "good public service."[8]

For reasons that remain unclear to this day, Uncle Charley's sons were less distinguished. Two of them met tragic ends. According to family lore, Thomas Klepzig, a commercial fisherman, perished by foul means; he had drowned in a Texas bayou with his hands tied behind his back. A second son, Robert, a bachelor, lived in a cellar up on the "old Shehee place" in Pin Oak Hollow. He was "so fat that he could hardly keep his eyes open." He died unheroically when he fell out of his springboard wagon while riding up Open Hollow. One of the wagon's wheels ran over his head.

Two other of Uncle Charley's sons evaded the draft during the Great War. When the United States entered World War I in 1917, both Alonzo and Oliver fled Shannon County. Under the assumed name of James Yates, Alonzo eventually settled down near Portland, Oregon, married, and had five or six children. Not until some twenty years later did his new family learn of his real name.

In the meantime, Oliver, the other son, assumed the alias of James Williams and for many years worked for a traveling circus. Oliver either inherited or bought the small farm of his mother, Keziah (a Rader and my great-aunt). Oliver returned to Shannon County now and then for visits and regaled his kinfolk with exciting tales of the outside world. When he was away as a circus roustabout, he welcomed a series of relatives to live in his small bungalow. It was in 1944 that my immediate family lived a few months in Oliver's place before we moved on to the goat farm near West Plains.

Oliver's house was unlike most of those in the neighborhood. It was a stud-frame rather than a log or "sawmill" house. As a nine-year-old, I marveled at one of its conveniences; rather than dropping a bucket tied to a rope into the well to retrieve water, Oscar had a hand pump. In addition, his house had a separate kitchen and dining room, a living room, and two bedrooms. Hanging on the walls in virtually every room were large, framed lithographs—not of family members but of famed historic scenes or of distinguished personalities!

Why did Oliver display these pictures? It could be that he consciously or unconsciously displayed the pictures as evidence of both his personal success and his pride in being an American citizen. Perhaps he regretted his earlier decision to avoid the draft and wanted to impress others with his affection for the United States.

~

Along with watching PBS's *Masterpiece Theater*, which routinely features English country houses with paintings of ancestors hanging on their interior walls, Oliver's pictures got me thinking more generally about heirlooms in the Ozarks. I cannot vouch for all Ozarks families, but what is striking about my own immediate and extended family is the absence of heirlooms. Few members of my family exhibited in their homes or elsewhere very many treasured material objects that ancestors had passed down to them and that might have strengthened their claims to having been a family of some historic significance.

I begin with an inventory of my immediate family's memorabilia. Neither my sister Ada nor I can recall a single material item—not a dress, a photograph album, a musical instrument, not even a book—that Mom inherited from her parents or her other ancestors. Doubtlessly the size of the family—eleven children—and the family's impoverishment partly account for this. Maybe one or more of Mom's siblings did possess an heirloom or two, but I have no evidence that they did.

Still, the Eddings family was historically conscious. Mom and at least a couple of her sisters tried to preserve some of the family's history by either passing it on to later generations orally or in writing. Aunt Ruth Eddings Shelton even did a twenty-or-so-page (typed) history of her father's side of the family. I also vaguely recall as a child visiting a cemetery on Memorial Day and decorating the graves of some of Mom's ancestors. In addition, surviving to this day is a large collection of family photographs of her family (many of them available on the internet) extending back to the first years of the twentieth century.

Although Pap did possess a few family heirlooms, he did not seem to treasure them much. The most used of the possessions handed down to him by his ancestors was Grandpa Sam's single-shot .22 rifle. But even in this instance, he employed it sparingly. In hunting, listening to his hounds track and tree a coon was far more fulfilling for him than the kill itself. Along with his sons and I think later his grandsons, he also used it occasionally to shoot squirrels, for target practice, and to kill hogs before butchering them. When not in use, he always hung it high, out of reach of inquisitive children. As far as my siblings and I can remember, he never attached any historic significance to the rifle. Illustrative of this point: When one of his grandchildren, Stace, turned four or five years old, he sawed off part of the stock of the rifle so that it was short enough for the youngster to shoot it!

Another of Grandpa Sam's former possessions was a fiddle. From adolescence through the 1930s, Grandpa had been an avid fiddle player and singer. He loved to render folk ballads such as "Sally Goodin," which had originated in Northern Ireland. Pap himself learned to play a little and, upon Grandpa's death in 1950, inherited his fiddle, but I do not recall him ever playing a complete song on the fiddle. And apparently sometime in the 1950s, after I had left home, he threw the fiddle away. It may have well been beyond repair by this time. In roughly the same time frame, he also got rid of Grandma Ada Rader's deteriorating sidesaddle.

In the meantime, Mom apparently decided that she should strive to preserve a cache of family memorabilia. She wrote two short accounts of her childhood in McHenry Hollow, kept some family photographs, and maintained one or more scrapbooks of her family's achievements. But alas, when she passed away in 1991, her children failed to preserve most of her treasured possessions.

~

In 1981, one of my distant cousins back in Kentucky, J. Anderson Childress, put the question this way: Why was it that "there were never kept within the clan heirlooms or keepsakes such as other families are likely to keep?"[9] To dismiss poverty as an answer would be a serious mistake, but I want also to suggest that the Childress clan and its descendants (including the Raders on Mahans Creek) experienced little need to employ material objects as evidence of who they were. In short, their identity rested firmly on the family's dense and intimate kinship network—in other words, in a complex set of relationships grounded in a specific place.

11

"My ___, She Is Holding a Python!"

I developed a dislike for snakes at an early age. My parents and neighbors repeatedly warned us children, "Beware of copperheads and cottonmouths!" If bitten by one, you could die, they said. I soon learned that unlike rattlesnakes, neither copperheads nor water moccasins (cottonmouths that were said to reside in Mahans Creek) played fair. They gave you no warning of when they were about to strike. Indeed, you might not even see them before becoming a victim of their deadly venom.

Childhood stories and experience with snakes reinforced my anxieties. Pap's best friend on Mahans Creek, his cousin Dave Pummill, had once stuck his hand under a rock looking for fish worms; a copperhead bit one of his fingers and he nearly died, at least according to family lore. And then, there was my more direct encounters with snakes. One morning at the cabin on Mahans Creek, we heard hens loudly squawking in the chicken house. Pap went to investigate and came out of the house with a large black snake wrapped around his neck. He threw the snake on the ground and killed it. The shape of the snake's body was grotesque, for it had swallowed several chicken eggs without the shells bursting. That image was unforgettable.

Neither did a couple of childhood experiences with copperheads do anything to allay my dislike of snakes. In the first, at our cabin on Mahans Creek, Pap, who at least in the summertime always relieved himself by stepping outside before going to bed, stepped barefooted on a snake. Fortunately unbitten, he grabbed a nearby stick of wood and beat the snake to death. It was a copperhead! At about the same time when Mike and I were four or five years old and walking about the farm, one of our dogs, a mutt, started barking a few steps in front of us. As Pap rushed across the field toward us, a copperhead struck the mutt on his nose. The copperhead then slithered away into the tall grass. The eyes of the poor dog swelled shut and the distressed animal fell into a deep fever. To relieve his misery, Pap shot him the next day. He told us the mutt might have saved our lives.

Because from time to time the family was desperately in need of cash, Pap would look for work in other places—for example, as a roustabout in the oil fields of Illinois or as an electrician in Kansas—leaving behind Mom with two small children, Mike and me. On one dark evening while we were sitting in the main room of our cabin, which was lit only by a coal oil lamp, Mom spotted a copperhead slithering under the front door. I remember that she was somehow able to shoo the snake back outside. She then stuffed a sheet under the door to block any further intrusions. All of these experiences I sometimes converted into a childhood nightmare. Where the original county road crossed our farm on Mahans Creek, I repeatedly dreamed of a gigantic serpent that stretched across the entire road. Before the serpent bit anyone or wrapped itself around anyone, I awakened in terror.

Living on farms first in Shannon and then later in Howell Counties, I continued to encounter snakes. At some point, I learned that not all snakes were dangerous and indeed that they assisted in ridding farm barns of rats and mice. Furthermore, I am unsure that I ever fully accepted the idea that a serpent, by persuading Eve to eat the forbidden fruit in exchange for her becoming like God, had been responsible for humans thereafter suffering the burden of original sin. In fact, at some point in my life, I began to sympathize with Eve. Who would not be tempted to eat an apple that thereby promised so much?

～

Once off the farm and living outside the Ozarks, snakes subsided in importance for me until an incident involving my eight- or nine-year-old daughter Anne. As it happened, my wife, Barbara, and I took our children to a wildlife presentation at the Children's Zoo in Lincoln, Nebraska. A presenter came on stage with an eight-foot-or-so python wrapped around his body. He explained that although pythons killed their prey by coiling their bodies tightly around them, contrary to popular opinion, this python as well as other snakes were not slimy and that he had no fear of being bitten or squeezed to death by it. At the end of his presentation, he asked if any of the numerous children present would like to hold the python.

Figure 9. Anne Rader, my irrepressible daughter, in about 1970. Today she is a pathologist practicing in Portland, Oregon. Courtesy of the author.

Instantly, without consulting with or obtaining permission from her parents (her usual mode of operation), Anne leaped up from her chair and ran forward. The snake handler turned the viper over to her. Fearlessly, as she proudly stood there, the python curled its long body around her. Both Barbara and I were mortified. "My ___, she is holding a python!" I thought or maybe I said it aloud.

12

When I Kissed My Sister

You may be wondering what I, as an Ozarker in my fifties, was doing riding a bicycle and camping outdoors in western France. A fair question, but that is another story. On this trip in the 1990s, my son-in-law Ken Gatter, a mutual friend Jesse Boyd, and I arrived in the late afternoon at a small village in Brittany where we planned to take refreshments. The place at which we stopped not only offered libations but also served as a local recreation center. There, we observed six or seven teenaged boys shooting pool. At about five o'clock, the boys began to peel off. We presumed that they were heading home for their evening meals.

Accompanying each of their departures was a remarkable ritual. Each boy "kissed" each of the other boys! Well, it was not quite the same as the prolonged "French" kisses that you might see in the movies or soap operas. In fact, the boys did not embrace in a full-body hug either. Instead, as each boy left, he leaned in over the shoulder of each of the other boys separately and while barely embracing, both boys made a light or an imitation of a kiss. The duo then did the same thing over the other shoulder. Finally, they repeated the entire procedure. I later learned that the number of kisses varied in France according to region.

I already knew that the French sometimes behaved in strange ways, but the only times that I could remember witnessing roughly similar ceremonies in the Ozarks was when, in the midst of an exciting high school basketball game, a teenaged boy might touch a teammate with his hand to reassure him that he had his teammate's back. Adult men also routinely shook hands. Any physical gesture suggesting a special tie with a member of your own sex otherwise, however, was strictly taboo.

Friedrich Gerstacker, a German visitor to the Arkansas Ozarks in the 1830s and 1840s, reported that "I wouldn't go so far to say that the families of these backwoodsmen don't care for each other just as much as we do, but they demonstrated their affection seldom or never. Parents never kiss their children, nor brothers and sisters kiss one another."[10] Gerstacker's summary of physical distancing within families squared with my conclusions more than one hundred years later. Perhaps I exaggerate. For example, my wife, Barbara, remembers that one of my wide-eyed sisters, Alice, who was ten years old, sat on Pap's lap while we were discussing our proposed marriage.

Rarely did my family or our neighbors express feelings by crying. It was as if somewhere in the process of passing from childhood to adulthood, we had forgotten how to cry. Although deeply loved by his family members, I think that no one cried at Grandpa Rader's funeral in 1950. As adults, even as teenagers, we were stoics. I remember only one instance of my mother crying and then only briefly. Presuming that he could use the family car to get to work, Pap had left his pickup at a garage overnight in town for repairs. But alas, the next morning he learned that Mom intended to use the car to attend a women's extension club meeting. At least a few tears began to well from Mom's eyes. As I recall, they quickly worked out a solution that entailed Mom driving Pap to work. Like everyone else, adult Ozarkers do experience sadness. They just don't waste their emotions in crying about them.

Anyhow, all of this got me thinking, how did Ozarkers recognize and express their special affections to one another, or did they? Perhaps by nicknames. Nicknames abounded among the male but not usually the female members of my own extended family. Each of my grandfathers and my father acquired nicknames, which can be, onomastics tell us, a recognition of a peculiar physical trait or behavior, an expression of humor and/or affection, or a means of putting someone in their place.

Consider my paternal grandfather. He chose his own nickname. His proper name was Edward Martin Rader, but when a child, a visitor to the Rader cabin gave him a nickel "and a lot of attention." After that when asked what his name was, he responded, "Sam." The name stuck for his entire lifetime. Sam permitted informality in his own household. According to Hulbert "Hub," one of his sons, all of his sons were as likely as not to refer to him as Sam as they were to call him Pa or Dad. I recall when around his own children, my father referred to him as Pappy.

Likewise, my maternal grandfather was better known by his nickname, Raz, than he was by his formal name, Alford Asbury Eddings. How he acquired his nickname is unknown, but it is probably safe to infer that it came from his middle name of Asbury. Maybe it was simply a shortening of the word "raspberry," a red berry grown in the Ozarks. It could also reflect one of his important personality traits. Raz enjoyed nothing more than teasing or "razzing" me about my odd beliefs such as thinking that the earth was round and that it was part of a heliocentric solar system.

Sometimes the meaning of nicknames in Ozarks families was unmistakable. For example, my first cousins Jerome and Max at times (maybe not to his face) called their pa, my uncle Hub, Orders. An unusual nickname, indeed, but I presume that Uncle Hub subjected his sons to an unending set of orders. He repeatedly ordered them to "do this or that!" After all, there was always something to do on a small creek-bottom farm. Frankly, after having written this, I am not so sure that my interpretation of his nickname holds up. It doesn't correspond perfectly with what I remember about Uncle Hub's behavior. But remember that Uncle Hub did once upon a time execute a whipping of Delaware School's teenaged delinquents.

As the oldest of six siblings, I took it upon myself to become the main source of nicknames within my own immediate family. My mother became "Mamacita," my father "Pap," my younger brothers "Bert" and "Hutch," and my younger sisters "Ada Flamachetti" and "Aldusty." Why I did this, why other members of the family tolerated it, and why they themselves began to use the same nicknames is uncertain. Partly, I think, it was a frequently misguided effort on my part to evoke humor and perhaps draw attention from other members of my family about how clever I was.

It is also possible to construe a more generous interpretation of my behavior. Maybe, as with the kissing ritual displayed by the boys in Brittany's recreation center, nicknaming had something to do with the expression of affection for and shoring up of my family's special identity and solidarity. Perhaps for this reason, it came as something of a surprise to me to learn that other people in our neighborhood sometimes employed our in-family nicknames when talking about members of my family. I was uneasy with this. I preferred that they address my family members by their proper forenames.

Since leaving the Ozarks, I hesitantly if awkwardly began to alter the expression of feelings toward fellow family members. For example, I

Figure 10. Kissing my sister Alice Rader Smith, on the occasion of her marriage in 1969. Courtesy of the author.

gradually began to reciprocate the hugs of my wife and children. But no incident revealed this radical change in my behavior more vividly than a kiss that I bestowed on my youngest sister, Alice, upon the occasion of her marriage in 1969. Notice as well in the photograph Alice's utter surprise.

PART II

The People There Even Drank
Rainwater from Cisterns

You might expect that the rigors of the Great Depression of the 1930s would have abraded the ties that held the Mahans Creek neighborhood together. It makes sense to think that the harsh circumstances of the day would encourage an unrestrained individualism in which every family would fend for itself. Instead, the hard times served to rally at least some of the local farmers behind a richer and fuller neighborhood life, one stronger than had existed anytime since the timber boom early in the twentieth century.

Families began to visit one another more frequently, and the once-moribund New Harmony Baptist Church started holding services again. In the winter-spring of 1932, my uncle Hub Rader founded the Delaware Society of Very Common Farmers, an organization of young people that met monthly to provide rollicking "entertainment" for "the community of Delaware." The neighborhood revived the local baseball team, the Delaware Tumblebugs,* which began on Sundays to play nearby town teams. Finally, apart from the local school, the Faust country store, nursery, and post office located near the schoolhouse continued to serve as a focal point for neighborhood life.

---

*Named by Uncle Hub and reflecting his sense of humor, tumblebugs are a scarab beetle that roll dung into small balls, lays eggs in them, and then buries them in the ground.

The Great Depression brought the extended Rader-Pummill clan closer together.[1] Even when the better-off families themselves were facing adverse circumstances, they came to the aid of their more needy kinfolk. I know this because my immediate family was a major beneficiary of their generosity. Nothing may have been more important to our well-being than the part-time temporary jobs that kinfolk offered to Pap.

Let me cite a few examples. Adjacent to our little creek-bottom farm, distant cousins, the Smith brothers, from time to time employed Pap for a dollar a day to toil on their Mahans Creek farm. Over in Open Holler, Uncle Arthur Pummill asked Pap to join his son Dave in building a new barn. In 1932, Uncles Lawrence and Joe Pummill put Pap, along with several other family members, to work clearing a campground and building a clubhouse on their jointly owned farm down the creek. In the late 1930s and early '40s, Pap, along with his brother Gilbert worked several months for Joe in developing his new estate south of Eminence. They cleaned up the grounds, built one of the finer houses in the county, dug a fishpond, and constructed a tennis court. I suspect but do not know for certain that during especially difficult times, various family members also extended cash to my family.

During the hard times, not only did an informal family safety net spring into existence, but it also brought "the tribe," as they now described the extended Rader-Pummill clan, closer together in other respects. Each summer beginning in 1932 (first at Jim Rader's place and thereafter at the Pummill campground on Mahans Creek), they gathered for a three-or-four-day big family reunion of fifty or more members. Most of the women and children slept on the main floor of the cabin or its porch while the men slept outside or in some instances in tents scattered about the grounds.

A gala affair, the reunion not only offered opportunities for reconnecting to the singular place where the Pummills had lived as children but numerous occasions for the renewal of personal relationships among kinfolk otherwise separated by time and place. The senior Pummills were nothing if not storytellers; they regaled their younger counterparts with humorous accounts of family life in earlier times. Apart from eating together, organized activities included contests in marble playing, horseshoe pitching, bridge, and usually a baseball game. The 1936 reunion even scheduled a contest for the prettiest baby. The selection committee judiciously decided to award the first prize to all six of the babies present, one of whom happened to be a not-so-pretty me.

Most memorable of all were the evenings when the tribe gathered in the great room of the cabin. There, they listened attentively to Joe Pummill's monumental recitations from memory of long poems, they sang, and they danced. With my grandpa Sam playing the fiddle, Dave Pummill a base tub (a homemade instrument with a single string), and Hub Rader the French horn, square dancing was the favorite. Many years later, my cousin Gloria Dene Rader Fry fondly remembers that her uncle Lowell (Pap) taught her how to square and jig dance.

Equally perhaps even more effective in nurturing family bonds in the grim '30s was the publication of a monthly newsletter called *The Passerby*. At the beginning of each month, Everett Pummill, the school superintendent in Eureka, Missouri, solicited letters from family members. He then edited and paraphrased the contents and frequently added both historical and amusing comments of his own. Apart from trivia, good-natured gender and political sparring occupied a special place in the two-page, single-spaced, mimeographed newsletter. The senior Pummill brothers—all Republicans except perhaps Elva who had earlier been a Socialist candidate for office in Shannon County—chided the Raders for being Democrats. On one occasion, Sam Rader shot back that even though the Democrats might have been unsuccessful in restoring prosperity, they had at least succeeded in making beer legal. No doubt, on reading this retort, everyone chuckled, for Sam was a well-known teetotaler!

In the final year of the 1930s and in the early 1940s, close family ties began to unravel. A turning point came with the unexpected death of Everett Pummill from a heart attack in 1939. Like a punctured basketball, the air seemed suddenly to have gone out of the whole extended family enterprise. Reunions were discontinued, the family issued only one more edition of *The Passerby*, and American entrance into World War II in 1941, impinged, though in different ways, on the lives of everyone. In 1942, Joe and Lawrence Pummill sold the family farm on Mahans Creek, and many other families departed from the neighborhood to take wartime jobs elsewhere. Ironically, the trials of the Great Depression had encouraged family cohesiveness while the prosperity accompanying World War II, like a sledgehammer, had suddenly sundered it apart.

~

Still, even in World War II, there remained for us children Mahans Creek. Fed by springs, the clear-water creek rushed from one side of the narrow steep-sided hollow to the other, in some places carving out limestone bluffs and caves along the way. Dense stands of willows and towering sycamores grew along its banks. Pools usually no more than three feet deep emptied into stretches of fast-running water that ran only a few inches above the gravel and sand that comprised its bottom. Less accessible to predators, it was in these stretches that each year the yellow suckers spawned. During spawning season, the creek-bottom farmers gigged the suckers and their wives fried up messes of them for the family's supper.

By digging wells of only ten feet or so deep in the hollow's floor, the farmers tapped into a water-filled aquifer. Not only did the rock-lined wells furnish fresh, clear, cold drinking water, but the farm families also cooled and stored their milk, butter, and watermelons in them.

In the summers, Pap, his clothes soaked with sweat from farmwork, would finish his day by stripping off his overalls and underclothes and taking a dip in the always-cold creek. Whenever we could, Mike and I lollygagged naked in the creek. "There was always something to do on the creek," explained my first cousin Jerome Rader. For children, the creek's attractions even trumped the popular Saturday afternoon western films of the day. Another cousin, Arch Pummill, who like me spent his early years on the creek, recalled in 2010, almost ninety years later, that he "bitterly resented leaving the creek" and to that day had never forgiven his parents for moving the family to Pittsburg, Kansas in the early 1920s.[2] For us children, without going to heaven, living on the creek was as close to paradise as we could get.

Little did we understand that like Adam and Eve in the Garden of Eden after they had tasted the tree of knowledge, we were about to be thrust out of our idyllic homeland. (Not by God—at least directly). We didn't know that it had been hard enough to earn a living on the creek in the best of times, but to borrow a phrase from Charles Dickens, these were the worst of times. Not only was there the Great Depression of the 1930s but there was also the worst drought in the history of Shannon County. World War II brought a brief but incomplete respite from the hard times. In 1944, Pap finally gave up.

~

To make the move from Mahans Creek, Mom supervised loading our essential household items onto the bed of a neighbor's pickup truck. With stock racks attached to the bed so that it could hold more stuff, Mike and I rode atop of the load while Mom, our two younger brothers, and the driver crowded into the front seat. The driver guided the pickup carefully up the hillside and out of the Mahans Creek waterway. Because of the thirty-five-miles-per-hour speed limit that had been imposed by World War II, plus perhaps the pickup's worn-out tires, the driver proceeded slowly—across Shannon County westward into Howell County, Missouri. Along the way, you can imagine that viewers of this spectacle must have looked at the truck and its occupants with some surprise if not misgivings. About two hours later, we arrived at our new destination, a tiny hilltop farm of thirty acres in the Schneider neighborhood. Schneider was some five miles northeast of West Plains, Missouri, a town of about 4,500 people that served as the Howell County seat.

To Mike and me, our new home had little in common with our old place on Mahans Creek. Where were our kinfolk? Our grandpa Rader, our uncles, aunts, and cousins? Those who had saved us from the worst rigors of the Great Depression? Not a single relative lived in our new neighborhood.

The very name of the nearby town, West Plains, conjured up images of West Texas, of tumbleweeds bouncing across a windswept prairie, of dried-up creek runs, of swirling dust, and of a countryside bereft of all but a few scraggly trees. In some respects, reality corresponded to these images. While the area around the town had much more annual rainfall than West Texas, its gently sloping ridges, shallow valleys, and relative absence of trees resembled the Great Plains. Covered with bluestem prairie grass underlain by Jefferson City red clay, the area around what was to become West Plains had remained for the most part unsettled until the federal government began surveying it in 1848.

Except in the valleys, everywhere you looked—in the road cuts and drainage ditches, the Schneider schoolhouse playground, the pond banks, and as often as not the upturned soil of newly plowed ground—there was the ubiquitous red clay. Even the local toads were red. Equally if not more striking than the clay was the absence of clear-water streams, of springs, and of shallow wells. This part of Howell County was a land of sinkholes, ponds, and cisterns. The people here even drank rainwater from their cisterns.

The shock to us was not simply the new physical habitat. It was the sheer number of people living there. An approximation of the density of its population can be gained by comparing the population of Delaware Township in Shannon County—some 150 persons in 1945—with that of Sisson in Howell County—nearly 1,500—where we now lived. Although both were rural townships, there were no large swaths of unoccupied land in Sisson Township. A few families who owned farms in Gunter's Valley, which drained into the middle fork of the Eleven Point River, were moderately prosperous, but most of the people lived on tiny, rock-strewn farms on the hillsides. Many of them milked a small herd of Jersey cows and sold their unpasteurized milk to the local cheese factory. Since this income rarely met all the needs of growing families, adult household members often took full- or part-time jobs in West Plains, perhaps at the cheese or shoe factories, two of the major employers in town.

When we arrived there in 1944, Schneider had little to commend itself as an identifiable neighborhood. Unlike the Mahans Creek (or Delaware, as it was sometimes called) neighborhood, it had never been the site of a country store, a post office, or a church. As far as I can discover, it had never hosted a religious revival or sponsored a baseball team. True, a few members of old families had lived in the school district since the early twentieth century, but the only neighborhood-wide organization of any consequence was the one-room school itself, which had begun classes as early as 1883. A tantalizing scrap of evidence suggests that in 1909, some of the school's "scholars"—likely teenaged boys—may have behaved badly. In its meeting for August 24, 1909, the school board "requested [that the] teacher [a Miss Viola Sand] not to allow the scholars to leave [the] Play Grounds during noon or recess without permission from [the] teacher and also not to allow guns to be brought on School Grounds."[3] Whether Miss Sand, who also did the janitorial work for the school, was able to enforce these requests is unknown. One can presume it might have been difficult, for she was likely to have been only a year or so older than some of the students. Incidentally, the board also authorized the cleaning of the school's cistern.

Few anticipated that in the immediate post–World War II years, the Schneider neighborhood would suddenly spring to life. At the center of the new awakening was not only the school but also the founding of a church, later officially named the Berean Baptist Church. In 1946, the Southern Baptists in Howell County appointed a full-time missionary, a Brother Earl Lewis, who, at the urging of a longtime local family, scheduled a two-week revival in the schoolhouse. As I recall, it yielded nearly a dozen converts. In the wake of the revival, the county extension service organized a home-makers' club and a 4-H club in the neighborhood. With the founding of these organizations and neighbors visiting one another more frequently, the tempo of life in the neighborhood quickened.

A convergence of circumstances set the stage for Schneider's denser social life. One was the return of prosperity for at least a few of the families. These included the Bob Stevenson family as well as our own. Bob, who by the way, bore a striking resemblance to the author Robert Louis Stevenson, was the beneficiary of the GI Bill of Rights Act of 1944. He set up a small dairy farm adjacent to our second farm in Gunter's Valley. Lowell Rader, my father, was employed in West Plains as an electrician for Neathery Radio and Electric; this job, which initially paid him thirty-five dollars a week, guaranteed that our fast-growing family would have one of the higher cash incomes in the neighborhood. These families, among others, now had the financial wherewithal to underwrite social innovations while minimizing the risks involved. Both families played conspicuous roles in the newly created Berean Baptist Church as well as in the neighborhood's women extension club and the 4-H club.

The schoolhouse itself became the site of most of the neighborhood's burgeoning activities. Perhaps as in the past, the school routinely sched-uled pie suppers and sometimes plays performed by its students to pay for books and other necessities. To entertain and auction off the pies, the school sometimes either paid or obtained the voluntary services of local celebrities, among them Earl "Red" Hall, an auctioneer, and Porter Wagoner, who was later to become one of the nation's most popular country music entertainers. The church typically met there on both Sunday mornings and evenings as well as for prayer meetings on Wednesday nights; in addition, it held vacation Bible schools during the summers. The neighborhood's 4-H club, named by my mother as Helping Hands, met at the schoolhouse monthly.

Built in 1904, the balloon-framed schoolhouse could seat about forty children. The school ground itself was on an uneven hillside; still, the students managed to play workup softball on the west side, which slanted sharply out to the road running adjacent to the schoolhouse. Typical of such one-room schools, the one at Schneider had separate outdoor toilets for girls and boys. Apart from an absence of cleanliness, a glance at the inside walls of the boy's toilets revealed a startling fact, that Ozarkers were not lacking in scatological imagination. By glancing at the toilet's walls, schoolboys could not only find an array of shocking words but also receive tutelage in risqué behaviors. The school ground had a well with a pump. Attached to the pump's spigot was a dipper shared indiscriminately by students seeking to slake their thirst.

Unlike our more isolated situation on Mahans Creek, ties to town, specifically to West Plains, took on an added importance for my family. Pap's primary identity no longer sprang from farming but instead from his employment as an electrician who worked mostly in town. He routinely not only regaled us with reports of town life but also was the main conduit for the family's growing engagement in the nation's consumer society. It was from West Plains that we began to learn something of the heterogeneity—different social classes, religions, ethnicities, and races—of modern America. Later, high school attendance in West Plains also expanded our awareness of a world outside of our family and our neighborhood.

The following vignettes are set mostly in our new neighborhood of Schneider in Howell County, Missouri, between 1944 and 1950.

13

The Hilltop of the Dead

There was more, much more, to the story than our expulsion from the paradise of Mahans Creek and move to the goat farm in the red clay country around West Plains where people drank water from their cisterns. There was the goat farm itself. When we arrived there in the fall of 1944, we at once encountered the disgusting detritus of the house and yard's previous occupants. These included deposits of fecal matter scattered about in the house itself and in the yard from the family's children. (I later learned that the younger children ran around without diapers or other underclothes.) To the credit of my parents, they quickly and energetically set about cleaning the place up, a massive undertaking that included new wallpaper inside the house and a new paint job on the exterior of the house as well as a new front porch built by Pap.

This was not all. We soon discovered that we had moved to a hilltop of the dead. Scattered about the thirty-acre farm of brush and rocks was a grotesque scene. Bones—skulls, ribs, hip bones, shoulder blades, leg bones—almost everywhere. As far as we could tell, there were no human bones; instead, the remains were those of domesticated animals. Apparently, there had been sometime in the not too distant past a great disaster. Countless goats may have died from disease, starved to death, or a combination of the two. There was virtually no grass on the hilltop of the dead, only the blackjack leaves of the low-lying brush, which hardly offered an adequate diet for survival, even for the goats, who seemed willing to eat anything.

Despite living in the midst of this past horror, Pap was determined to try to make the best of it. He purchased some forty head of goats! The theory was, I think, that the goats would subsist mostly on the farm's brush, that Mike and I (though only ten or eleven years old) would milk them, and that we would sell the milk to new mothers who either did not or could not breastfeed their babies. (At the time in the late 1940s, it was popular for new mothers to abandon breastfeeding in favor of various artificial formulas, or the new babies could drink goat's milk which was said to be more digestible for babies than cow's milk.)

In the end, Pap's experiment failed. Keeping the goats fenced in even with good woven wire was nearly impossible. As with their predecessors, the goats did not thrive on the farm's brush; they required supplementary food. Finally, neither Mike nor I were enthusiastic or adept at milking the contrary animals. Unlike milk cows who usually welcomed the opportunity to eat some form of grain while being relieved of their milk, milking kicking goats, even though they enjoyed eating the grain, was no easy matter. Apart from putting "kickers" on their hind legs, one had to place one knee in front of the animal's rear legs to keep it from kicking over the pail into which you tried to squirt the milk. Apart from the difficulty of milking them, it may also be that the local demand for their milk was not great enough to sustain the experiment. In any case, Pap soon gave it up and sold the goats.

Still, ghosts of the past continued to loom over the goat farm. Not only did the bones strewn over the farm remain, but we learned that in earlier times, a basement west of our house had been covered with a ground-level roof of dirt with grass growing on top of it—in other words, camouflaged. Indeed, the goat farm had once been the site of a small moonshining operation. The fact that we lived on a place that had at one time possessed a nefarious reputation gave my brother Mike and me some immediate standing in our new neighborhood.

14

You Can't Take the Country Out of the Country Boy

Moving to the goat farm in Howell County failed to erase our longings for our idyllic playground on Mahans Creek. How could Mike and I forget those hot summer days when we peeled off our clothes, waded into the cold water of the spring-fed creek, felt the sand oozing up between our toes, and watched the minnows darting around our bare legs? Or digging into one of Grandpa's freshly grown watermelons?

Frequent return visits to the creek on weekends reinforced our nostalgia. Much to the annoyance of our younger siblings and perhaps our parents as well, when crossing the boundary marked by a sign announcing our arrival in Shannon County, Mike and I would loudly proclaim what we considered as salient fact: that even the air had suddenly improved!

Perhaps surprisingly, however, we did not fall into a deep melancholy. With a resilience characteristic of the young, we soon began exploring the unusual aspects of our new habitat. Unlike down on Mahans Creek, there were now neighbors nearby; we could even see a few hundred yards away the barn and house of two oldsters, Ma Huddleston and her brother, Uncle John. Before long, we discovered a patch of wild blueberries on their farm. There was a new school, which brought us face-to-face with a new teacher and a new set of students.

And there was religion. Although insofar as I can remember, we had never attended a religious service while living on Mahans Creek, perhaps because the church at Delaware had discontinued services, my parents suddenly decided that it was time that we "got" religion. At Southern Baptist revivals and church services held in the schoolhouse, we heard terrifying sermons about the prospects of going to hell or heaven. In time, the entire family became members of the newly established Berean Baptist Church. Every Sunday morning and night, frequently on Wednesday nights, and nightly during annual two-week revivals, we attended religious services.

Then perhaps most exciting of all was the lure of West Plains. Mike remembers that shortly after we had arrived in Howell County, Pap pointed out to us one evening an orange halo in the distant southwest. "That is the light coming from West Plains," Pap explained; the unusual light seemed to signal possibilities of radically new experiences. The very existence of such towns—at least of this size—was something new to us; up to this time, I am sure I could count on my fingers the times I had been in a town.

With our move to the goat farm, we began, however tentatively and incompletely, to bridge the yawning gap that separated town and country. Now, six days a week, Monday through Saturday, Pap returned from work in town with stories about settings and peoples unknown to us. Nearly every evening, he brought home some fresh groceries and a block of ice for the icebox. I remember that only he within the family was strong enough to wrestle the ice blocks into place.

In those first years, most exciting of all were our visits to town. On Saturday trading days or Monday's livestock auction, people, lots of them, far more people than I had ever seen before flocked onto the paved sidewalks and into the stores from the countryside. In town, there were even Black people! While staring in wonder at the moving crowds of people, I still have memories of drinking a Grapette (a grape soft drink of the day) and chewing on a carrot that I had bought with my own money. (Up to this day, friends occasionally tease me about my special fondness for carrots.)

The town offered other attractions. Baseball games, circuses, and above all else, the "picture show." At that time, a time before the intrusion of television, West Plains hosted two movie houses (plus later on, a drive-in movie), so we began with some regularity to attend the cowboy movies on Saturday afternoons. Cowboys, country singers, and baseball players became our new heroes. West Plains itself was the home of Bill Virdon, the big-league baseball player, and Porter Wagoner, the country music performer. Along with singing locally at pie suppers in Schneider, where I first heard him perform, and on the recently established local radio station KWPM, Porter was our butcher at the Vaughn grocery store on Washington Avenue. Since Pap traded there, he knew Porter, at least casually.

All of this having been said, Mike and I continued to be country boys, at least until we reached high school. But even then, an old country saying remained salient: "You can take the country boy to town, but you can't take the country out of the country boy."

15

Walking to School

I am sure that you have observed it: When you drive in the morning or the late afternoon through your neighborhood or across town, you are likely to encounter in the vicinity of the local schools a traffic jam. Parents, their cars stopped, blocking the street while they are either dropping off or picking up their children from school. Indeed, to avoid delays, my wife, Barbara, and I sometimes take longer, alternative routes to our destination points.

Although in terms of safety, there is much to commend in this practice, today's kids miss out on opportunities to brag about themselves to later generations. They will be unable to beguile their own children with tales of how they, in order to get back and forth to school, had to wade through deep snow in subfreezing weather. They will be unable to say that when they were kids, kids had to be tough.

The truth is, I suspect, older generations frequently exaggerate the trials that they encountered when they were children. Even though it is true that in the old days in the rural Ozarks, kids did for the most part walk back and forth to school, sometimes as far as a mile and a half or so, the truth is that neither my siblings nor I had much to brag about. Even in the wintertime, the weather in the Ozarks is usually mild.

In 1884, a writer for the local weekly, the *Current Wave*, in Eminence, made this point forcefully when he reported that a farmer from Illinois, one Andrew Phelps, decided that he had had his fill of life on Mahans Creek. Phelps "concluded to return to Illinois, and accordingly took a 'straight skoot' for the state of doubtful politics [i.e., Republican] and horizontal reduction [i.e., the flatlands], going down Shawnee [Creek] and [it] became cooler, an ominous soughing of the wind in the surrounding pines was heard, and, remember[ing] with a shiver the rigors of Illinois winters, he lost heart. He hitched up his team to the rear end of the wagon and came backwards to Mahan's Creek. There is no place like Shannon."[4]

But I digress. Much of the time, neither my siblings nor I walked all the way to school and back. When living on Mahans Creek, my family was technically in the Crescent (sometimes called Buckhart) school district. With the end of the timber boom, the district lost nearly all of its population so that by 1941 when I started school, the school had been shut down for several years. At that date, I think there were only three school-aged children in the district. Two of them came from a bootlegging family, the Bartons up in Open Holler.

Given these circumstances, the Crescent district hired Lufton Barton to transport us by car down Open Holler to the Delaware schoolhouse.

As a first grader, I merely had to walk over a steep hill to Open Holler to await the arrival of Lufton. He brought me back by way of the same route after school had closed in the afternoon. I suspect that Lufton's old car was unheated. On cold days, he would take the precaution of heating two large rocks in the family's kitchen oven, wrap them in blankets, and place them on the floorboard of the back seat. I remember fondly removing my shoes and warming my feet atop the warm rocks.

Figure 11. Schneider schoolchildren (1947?). Mike and Ben Rader from left to right in the front row. That Mike's shirt is hanging out over his pants below his sweater is something of a shock to me. By reputation, I was a far sloppier dresser than he was. Courtesy of the author.

Neither did I have a difficult time getting back and forth to Schneider School in Howell County. My siblings and I nearly always caught a ride by car from either Pap or the teacher for part or most of the way to school.

Still, we did walk part of the way, far enough each day to have experiences that most kids miss today. How many children have an opportunity in the fall to sample the not-very-sweet, tiny grapes that used to grow along country roads in Howell County? To watch a red fox after a night of hunting returning to its den in the morning? Or to observe the majesty of flight, as a formation of migrating geese? To watch a cow nursing her newborn calf?

There were also lurking dangers, some of which my parents never learned about. Once, a neighbor, Old Man Huffman, stopped Mike and me on our way to school. "How would you boys like to earn a dime?" he asked. A dime was a lot of money to us, so we said yes. He then explained our task. He needed the chimney of his wood-burning fireplace cleaned, but he was suffering from high blood pressure and feared that he might have a heart attack if he did it himself. For us to accomplish this feat, we were to climb a ladder to the top of the steeply pitched roof of his two-story house. He would then hoist up to us a long pole with a toe sack wrapped around one end. We were then to employ the pole as a plunger, forcing it up and down in the chimney until it had removed the soot. This was a project that, in retrospect, seemed destined for disaster. One foot on each side of the roof and only ten years old, I could barely lift the plunger let alone maintain my balance while driving it up and down inside the chimney. Finally, in utter frustration with my feeble efforts, Old Man Huffman himself climbed up to the roof and plunged his chimney. Even though we had failed to clean his chimney, he paid us a dime anyway. And he did not have a heart attack, at least not right away.

On another occasion, as we were walking across one of Old Man Huffman's fields, we saw one of our mongrel dogs who was chasing a rabbit suddenly disappear. As we approached the spot where we had last seen him, we found that overnight, the bottom had fallen out of part of the field. Our dog had fallen into a perfectly round steep-sided sinkhole of some fifteen feet deep or so. As we peered down into the hole, we heard the mutt whimper in pain, but we could do nothing for the distressed animal. We decided to return home and tell Pap what had happened. A practical man, he took down his ancient .22 rifle from the pegs above the kitchen door and we walked over to the sinkhole. Pap carefully aimed the rifle and shot the mutt in the head, instantly relieving him of his pain.

But transcending all of these experiences for my brother Mike and me was the unstructured time that walking to and fro to school afforded us to engage in uninhibited talk. Even as preteenagers, virtually no subject was off limits. We allowed our imaginations to roam freely, even to the extent of creating scenarios in which we performed heroic feats that would have made the Babe himself envious.

I am reasonably sure that these flights of fantasy contributed a lot to what Mike and I later became—he a highly successful electrical contractor and me a professional storyteller of the past—that is, a historian.

16

When Miss Delores Read Us a Novel

Finishing one chapter each time, it took Miss Delores, our eighteen-year-old teacher, forty-five days to read us a novel. ("Us" refers to the twenty-seven students spread out in ages from five to fifteen at Schneider's one-room rural school in 1946.) She opened the book and began reading promptly at 1:00 p.m., after we had eaten a cold lunch and perhaps played a game of "workup" softball. At the time, this did not surprise me. As a fifth grader, I welcomed the respite from studies and the opportunity to listen to an exciting story. But today, I see this event quite differently.

Let me set the scene in greater depth. First, I very much doubt that the reading of any novel was part of the approved curriculum of Missouri's educational authorities in 1945–46. After all, it was the teacher's main duty to teach the students how to read, not to keep them occupied by reading to them. From the standpoint of the professional educators and, needless to add, probably many of the neighborhood's parents, there was an additional issue. The novel Miss Delores chose to read was not what you might expect; be assured it was not Harold Bell Wright's *Shepherd of the Hills* (1907) or Mark Twain's *Adventures of Tom Sawyer* (1876).

Instead, it was Harriet Beecher Stowe's *Uncle Tom's Cabin* (1852), one of the most banned books in American history. It explicitly assaulted racial slavery in America before the Civil War and implicitly the new racial apartheid that was put in place in the wake of Reconstruction. The heroic protagonist of the book was a Black slave, the Christlike Uncle Tom, while the stereotypical villain was the devil-like Simon Legree, a white slaveholder. When it was first published in 1852, there was no end of slavery in sight, but its clear-cut message not only helped to mobilize public opinion in both North and South in favor of war but continued to resonate down to the present.

To be sure, there were those, particularly African Americans themselves, who were seeking an end the nation's racial injustice in 1946, but one would be hard-pressed to find any whites in the Ozarks at the forefront of such a campaign. Was Miss Delores an exception? I don't know, but I do know that hearing Stowe's moving exposure of the evils of slavery and of racism left indelible impressions on two of her young students: my brother Mike and me.

17

The Punishment of Curley Pliler

Mike and I were building miniature roads in the dirt of our peach orchard on the goat farm when blood-curdling screams suddenly interrupted the country silence. Only about one hundred yards away, we saw Curley Pliler, one of Ma Huddleston's farmworkers, rifle in hand, marching Dave Barnes, another of Ma's farmhands, down the lane to Ma's house. Curley was yelling at Dave, "I am going to kill you, you son of a bitch!" With tears rolling down his face, Dave bawled like a hungry calf. He was a sorry-looking mess.

Scared, we rushed from the peach orchard to the house to tell Pap, who had just arrived home from work. Pap and Mom discussed what to do. Against Mom's judgment but determined as best he could to prevent a murder, Pap decided to walk unarmed down to Ma's place. In the meantime, we waited anxiously, fearing that at any moment we might hear one or more gunshots.

After what seemed like hours, much to our relief, Pap finally returned. How he talked Curley Pliler out of killing Dave Barnes, I will never know. Regardless, with this incident, my esteem for Pap's bravery soared. If a boy needs a personal hero, Pap was now mine.

The next morning at about 7:30 a.m., a strange thing happened. Per usual, after breakfast Pap prepared to drive into West Plains to work. There, awaiting his departure was Curley Pliler! Politely, Curley asked Pap if he could catch a ride into town with him. Pap replied, "Yes, but you will have to ride outside standing on the running board of the car."

I never asked Pap to explain why he insisted that Curley ride on the running board, but it seemed like an appropriate punishment for the threat that Curley had posed to the neighborhood's peace. In any event, thus was the spectacle and the punishment. Pap inside the warm car and Curley standing on the running board outside the car on a frosty morning in short sleeves. On the six-mile trip into West Plains, Curley surely shivered, more than once. Perhaps it was not coincidental that Curley later served time in the Missouri State Penitentiary after a nonlethal gunfight with one of his cousins.

18

When We Danced Naked in the Rain

Convenience usually trumped privacy when we lived in the log house down on Mahans Creek. After all, steep hills and trees shielded our behavior from our neighbors, and we rarely had visitors. We had no indoor toilet; so, at least in the case of the males in the family, they frequently relieved themselves outdoors. And then, there was the cabin itself, which made the preservation of modesty difficult. Initially, it consisted of only a small kitchen, a storage room, and a living room. The living room also served as a bedroom for Mom, Pap, Mike, and me.

I didn't see anything unusual about this arrangement until one evening when Mike and I (as five- or six-year-olds) began to strip off our clothes in preparation for bed. We had a visitor that night, a slightly older first cousin. I glanced up to find him cowering behind the couch half-naked. It then dawned on me that he was embarrassed about removing his clothes in front of Mom. Why? After all, Mom was just Mom.

The creek itself encouraged casual attitudes toward nudity. After a hard day's work in the sweltering summertime, Pap himself routinely discarded his sweaty overalls and underclothes and took a dip in the always-cold creek. (His pappy and his brothers had a tradition of doing this.) The whole family frequently followed Pap—Mike and I naked but Mom wearing a dress. On other occasions, Mike and I seized on every opportunity we could to skinny-dip in the creek. With the arrival of two younger brothers in the 1940s, Mom took advantage of our love of wallowing in the creek. She insisted that we had to wash out the soiled diapers of our baby brothers before we could go "swimming." But even this unpleasant task did not deter us, at least not for long.

When we moved to the hilltop farm in Howell County in 1944, we had no direct access to a creek, but about a mile or so away from our house was what we called the blue hole, a deep hole in the normally dry-water creek in Gunter's Valley. Here, along with some neighboring boys, we would swim naked in the summer. By this time, adding to the excitement of the occasion was the fact that we were becoming adolescents and the possibility (fed by rumors or maybe threats) that the local girls in the neighborhood were planning on peeking in on our escapades. I don't recall that they ever did. Perhaps it was simply wishful thinking on our part.

In the meantime, our family had moved to yet another farm, a half mile from the county road and surrounded by dense woods. There was no year-round creek there either, but still, when it rained in the summertime, my brother Mike and I took off our clothes and danced (maybe "pranced" is the more accurate word) about the yard. Not only did we exhilarate in the physical freedom from constraining clothes but also in the pleasant sensations of warm rainwater falling on and trickling down our bare skins. The only witnesses of our rain dance were my mom and our two youngest brothers. Insofar as I can remember, Mom looked on our rain dance with bemused tolerance. That is until two little sisters joined the family circle. When my sisters were four or five, Mom put a stop to our dancing naked in the rain.

19

How Harry Caray Punctured Our Innocence

I must have been full of myself on December 8, 1941, when as a six-year-old first grader, I announced to the Delaware School that the Japanese had bombed Pearl Harbor. As I recall, neither Miss Eulah, the teacher, nor any of my classmates quite believed me, even though I was simply reporting what I had heard on my family's battery-powered radio the previous day. Why were my fellow students surprised? I suppose that either their families did not own a radio or for some other reason, my classmates had not heard the shattering news.

A measure of the importance of my announcement for me personally can be gathered from subsequent events. For shortly thereafter, I became something of a news correspondent for the whole one-room school. Before school commenced each morning, Miss Eulah permitted or perhaps encouraged me to explain and draw maps illustrating the course of the war on the blackboard. Families on Mahans Creek did not escape the impact of the war in other respects. As with the remainder of the nation, families faced the rationing of consumer goods, purchased savings stamps (in small quantities for sure), some family members volunteered or were drafted into military service, and I remember saving aluminum cans and empty toothpaste tubes. Pap even contributed a dollar to a fund that furnished American troops with cigarettes.

During the early 1940s, my younger brother Mike and I became avid radio listeners. We especially relished the late-afternoon serials broadcast by KMOX, a powerful AM radio station in Saint Louis. These included, as I recall, Amos 'n' Andy, Fibber McGee and Molly, Jack Armstrong: The All-American Boy, the Green Hornet, and Lum and Abner. Topping all others was the Lone Ranger. Even to this day, upon hearing the *William Tell* overture, I conjure up heroic images of an anonymous masked man, of his powerful horse Silver, of his loyal sidekick, Tonto, and of their inevitable triumph of good over evil. Perhaps it was this show more than anything else that propelled me into the historical profession.

Our love affair with radio serials continued after we had moved to the Schneider neighborhood in 1944, but it took a decided turn three years later when Robert "Bob" Neathery, a co-owner of the electric company for which Pap worked, founded radio station KWPM in West Plains. At first, Bob let anyone perform on the air for free whether they had a sponsor or not. Neathery Radio and Electric Company itself had an early morning program that broadcast from the courthouse square. On one occasion, even Pap performed "Old Dan Tucker" for them.

From the start, taking as his model the legendary country singer Hank Williams, Porter Wagoner sang from the Vaughn grocery store butcher shop where he worked as a meat cutter. Wagoner even recorded Williams's epic "Love Sick Blues" while in West Plains. Upon hearing Wagoner, Joe Fite, the local Trailways bus driver, commended the crooner to the staff of radio station KWTO in Springfield. From there, Wagoner, as both a songwriter and performer, achieved national renown when he moved on to the Ozark Jubilee in Springfield, the Grand Ole Opry in Nashville, and finally to his own long-running television show that featured his duets with Dolly Parton.

But it was not Porter Wagoner or any other of KWPM's performers who so infatuated Mike and me. It was listening to Harry Caray, the voice of the Saint Louis Cardinals baseball team. It is difficult to exaggerate the importance of Caray in nurturing an emotional attachment to the Cardinals among thousands of fans who listened to his broadcasts on some 120 AM radio stations scattered over nine states. On humid summer weekends, the arrival in Saint Louis of busloads of Cardinals fans from towns across the listening area provided visible testimony of Caray's skill in building team loyalty. Accurately described as "a fan behind the mic," Caray was renowned for his dramatic pet phrases: "It might be . . . it could be . . . it is! A home run," "Swung on and missed," "Holy cow!" and many others. No team announcer pulled harder for the home team than Harry. Overnight, Mike and I became converts to Cardinals baseball. When working out in the fields, we successfully convinced Mom to listen to the games and to keep us informed of anything important that happened while the game was in progress.

Caray was also a beer salesman with few peers. He not only allegedly drank beer while broadcasting, but he also urged his listeners to do the same. At first, he shilled his sponsor, Griesedieck Brothers of Saint Louis, as the greatest beer ever brewed, but imagine our surprise when August Busch, the owner of Anheuser-Busch Brewery in Saint Louis, purchased the Cardinals in 1953. Without missing a beat, Caray now informed us that Budweiser, the product of Anheuser-Busch, was the "King of Beers"! I don't think that he ever mentioned on the radio Griesedieck Brothers beer again.

Nor was Harry Caray loyal to the Cardinals either! In 1969, he left Saint Louis to become an announcer first for the Oakland Athletics, then for the Chicago White Sox for eleven seasons, and finally for the Chicago Cubs from 1982 to 1997. Indeed, Harry Caray's manifest disloyalty, when combined with our other experiences, may have dealt irretrievable blows to our youthful innocence. It surely should have.

20

"Let There Be Light"

"And God said, 'Let there be light.' And God saw that the light was good, and he separated the light from the darkness" (Genesis 1:3). In the Judeo-Christian tradition, this was an epochal moment in the history of creation, not only because God separated light from darkness but also because he attributed to light goodness. Since then, light has stood for the positive, for enlightenment or knowledge, hope, civilization, and morality, while darkness has evoked ignorance, fear, evil, savagery, and death.

As an example of light's larger meaning, consider the iconic painting "Boyhood of Lincoln" (1868) by Eastman Johnson. In Johnson's rendering, the shadows surrounding young Lincoln merge into darkness, but the light from the fireplace, albeit a single, fragile source, offers the lad an escape from darkness. For boy Lincoln could now read and by so doing, improve himself. The fireplace light provided him with the means to seize upon the opportunities available in nineteenth-century America to become a self-made man of great consequence.

Similar thinking apparently lurked in the thinking of my great-uncle Everett Pummill. Uncle Everett recalled that when he was a youngster down on Mahans Creek in the late nineteenth century, he and his brothers had "studied many nights by the light from the big fireplace fed with pine knots gathered from the hills."[5] The light cast by the big fireplace, Uncle Everett suggested, was essential in their quest to "do great things." And in time, the Pummill boys did indeed achieve great things.

Alas, although I likewise was born and lived on the same creek as the Pummills, I missed out as a beneficiary of light from a fireplace. Fireplaces scared Pap. He knew that they had been the cause of fires that burned down too many of the houses in the neighborhood. Besides, they were not a very efficient source of heat. You could warm yourself on one side, but your reverse side would remain cold. In any event, every time the family moved into a new place, Pap at once replaced the fireplace with a wood-burning stove.

Still, the family did "let there be light," not from a fireplace but from kerosene lamps. At some point in the family's history, we also bought an Aladdin lamp. Albeit more fragile and expensive than a kerosene lamp, the Aladdin lamp, since it cast a much brighter and whiter light, was far more satisfactory for reading. Indeed, as I recall, it may have been as good a source of light as a hundred-watt electric bulb.

When Pap took a job as an electrician in West Plains in 1944, we had no electricity in our home on the goat farm. But Pap, who was something of a jack of all trades, shortly after we moved there devised us a home lighting system by hooking up batteries to a generator that was powered by gasoline washing machine motor. In order to keep the batteries charged, my recollection is that we had to run the noisy motor for an hour or so nearly every night. Perhaps needless to add, it did not generate enough energy to power a refrigerator or any other kind of motor.

Finally, in 1950 I think it was, when I was nearly fifteen years old, the Rural Electrification Administration (commonly known as the REA by rural folk) brought electric lighting to our second farm in Howell County. Although Pap welcomed the new marvel, he didn't like the way that the REA did it. With chain saws, the REA crew sliced a thirty-foot right-of-way through the middle of the woods across the valley from our home; the path violated the natural seamlessness of the woods. That the REA planted only one pole in the valley itself (and that one in a fencerow) only partly relieved Pap's dissatisfaction. In any case, within days, we could switch on and off electric lights both in our house and in our barn. And now we even had an electric-powered refrigerator and radio.

It came as close to a miracle as anything we had ever experienced.

21

An Ozarks Book Burning

My mom was a reader. This, despite the fact that as a child, her family owned only a Bible and perhaps an almanac and that no one else in her immediate family read much. School was also something of an anathema to her thirteen-member branch-water family. After all, she even finished high school! All of her family members except her struggled with mastering basic spelling and grammar.

Exactly what hooked Mom on reading is unclear, but from a letter that she wrote to my daughter many years later, I do know something about her memories as a childhood reader. She wrote that a neighbor who lived in a nearby holler loaned her armloads of books to read. Her favorite authors were Gene Stratton-Porter and Zane Grey, two popular novelists of the early twentieth century.

The experience of reading these romantic authors, she observed, profoundly affected her entire life. Although the Ozarks were in some senses far removed from the prairie, desert, and mountainous settings of Zane Grey's books, she identified with Grey's lonely protagonists, especially with the girls and women, who not only braved the storm and stress of daily living but also brought a modicum of civilization to the primitive West. Even more to her liking was Stratton-Porter, whom incidentally she mistakenly thought was a male author. Porter's child characters lived in the remote Indiana countryside. Lonely and shy, with a bit of luck and lots of pluck, they in time transcended these handicaps. Such was her love of Stratton-Porter that she bestowed upon her firstborn (me) the middle name of Gene and upon her fourth-born (Howard) the middle name of Stratton.

I knew virtually nothing about her reading habits from those childhood days until I myself became a voracious reader some fifteen years later.

Figure 12. Lydia Eddings Rader, my mom and a fellow reader, in 1961. Courtesy of the author.

When I was a nine-year-old third grader, she insisted (despite the family's straitened financial circumstances) that we subscribe to the Springfield, Missouri *Leader and Press*, a daily newspaper; shortly thereafter, we also began taking the monthly *National Geographic* magazine and receiving condensed books monthly from the Reader's Digest book club. Suddenly, as I recall, reading materials that she and I both read flooded into our household.

Another turning point in our joint reading came when I entered high school. It was then that we began reading books assigned by my English teachers. Among them, as I remember, was Joseph Conrad's *Lord Jim*, which, while romantic and fulsome with adventure, is far more complex and sophisticated than the books of Grey or Stratton-Porter. In my sophomore year in high school, I also discovered a drugstore on Washington Avenue in West Plains that sold cheap paperbacks, sometimes for a nickel. These books opened up another whole world to my mom and me, including access to some authors, such as Frank Yerby and Erskine Caldwell, who, though certainly not as explicit as later novelists, were suggestive enough that it required only a little imagination for the reader to conclude that some kind of naughty, risqué acts were taking place. I do not remember that my mother sought to censure any of my reading. Indeed, it was from my mom rather than Pap that I first learned about the rudiments of birth control.

Upon returning home after having been away to college for a few years, I learned that nearly all of my cheap paperbacks had been the victims of a book burning! I am quite certain that this episode bore little resemblance to historic book burnings. To, for example, Girolamo Savonarola's "bonfire of the vanities," which you may remember from your Western civilization course entailed the burning of thousands of books (including the libertine treatises of Giovanni Boccaccio). It was said that Boccaccio tempted fifteenth-century Florentines to engage in orgies of immoral behavior. No, instead of a formal book burning, Mom had simply instructed one of my brothers to bring all of my old paperbacks into the backyard, there to rip them apart and to burn them. Insofar as I know, no ritual or speeches accompanied this occasion and that only my brother and perhaps Mom witnessed the event.

To be sure, the old paperbacks had deteriorated badly and reeked with mustiness, but I was none too happy when I learned of their fates. "Why did you burn my books?" I demanded of Mom. She smiled and calmly replied, "Remember that you have two younger sisters!" I am uncertain how this response should be interpreted since Mom had not censored any of my reading, but I am guessing that she, along with many other Ozarkers of the day, presumed that it was a more serious matter for girls to be corrupted by salacious literature than it was for boys.

PART III

"I Would Choose to Live in Town or beside a Busy County Road"

When he set his mind to it, Lowell "Pap" Rader could be quite convincing. Consider what happened to our family in 1949 when he pointed out to Lydia (Mom) the merits of buying a new farm.

Although the house and acreage that we owned and presently occupied was satisfactory as a place to live, he observed, it hardly qualified as a real Ozarks farm. Hilly, covered with brush, and strewn with rocks, its measly thirty acres was not even suited to goats, let alone pigs or cows. On the other hand, no one could dispute that the for-sale place, the old Bertha Cole farm, was a genuine farm. On the upper reaches of Gunter's Valley, it sported about eighty acres of pasture and bottomland plus about fifty acres of woodland. By purchasing it, the Rader family could at once claim a higher standing in the Schneider neighborhood. In the meantime, we sold the farm down on Mahans Creek to Pap's brother Merle.

Pap made his case on other grounds. While he would continue working in West Plains as an electrician, he reassured his eight-member family, we would not have to worry about basic sustenance. But the sweetest part of the proposal from Pap's perspective was the prospect of putting my brother and me to work. Since his two oldest sons were on the cusp of becoming strapping teenagers, he reasoned, they not only would gain the invaluable work experience that arose from farming, but they could also contribute directly to the family's upkeep. This was not all. My mom would be the

Figure 13. Our new farmhouse in Gunter's Valley in Howell County, Missouri. Courtesy of the author.

beneficiary of a more "modern" two-story house, one with stud (rather than raw logs) framing; the house had a separate kitchen and three separate bedrooms. And, finally, there was the bonus of the place being picturesque, for the house stood atop a knoll overlooking on three sides the verdant fields below.

Pap's scenario, at least as I recall it many years later, neglected to explore one drawback. The house of the thirty-acre place in which we presently lived was next to a regularly graded county road. Neighbors drove by it on their way to town, school, or church and even sometimes stopped by for a chat. When we first moved there in 1944, had it not been for a drop-in neighbor informing us that the local one-room school was in session, my brother and I would have missed more than one week of school. Not only that but we had a nearby neighbor, Ma Huddleston, who with her brother Uncle John and her hired hand, lived only a couple of hundred yards down the road. As our family owned a radio, I still remember rushing down to her house to inform her of the death of President Franklin D. Roosevelt in 1945.

The place Pap wanted to buy, on the other hand, was a half mile off the county road. Even by Ozarks standards, there was nothing quite like driving the narrow, bumpy road into the new farm. Dense woods cast long, dark, even ominous shadows across the roadway. (As our car bounced off the limestone outcroppings and loose rocks many years later, upon experiencing the road for the first time, my four-year-old son's eyes widened in utter amazement. "Gol-ly!" he repeatedly exclaimed.) True, when emerging at the other end of the road, one encountered the welcoming arms of open vistas, but beyond them were the far less inviting woods. There were woods in every direction—not a single neighbor's house in sight. Unless by mistake or specific design, no one ever drove into the place.

Still, Pap's scenario was not completely amiss. While he at best enjoyed only modest success in transforming my brother and me into hardworking farmhands, my mom welcomed living in a more spacious house. And no doubt, countless hours of caring for a large family drove away at least some of her potential loneliness. She finally learned to drive a car, which allowed her to commune more with nonfamily members and join more easily in such neighborhood activities as church, school, home extension, and 4-H club.

But there must have been moments, perhaps many of them, when, upon finding herself hour after hour without any adult companionship, the chilling realization of where she lived hit her with full force. As one year stacked upon another—even though Mom rarely complained about anything—she, with a tight smile, told family members that if she were able to live her life over again, she would choose to reside in town or in a house beside a busy county road.

The following vignettes are set in the first place on our new farm in Gunter's Valley between about 1949 and about 1953. It concludes with a vignette on my experience working, attending college, and living in Wichita, Kansas between 1953 and 1957.

22

An Ozarks Rite of Passage

To become a 4-H club member, I had to have a project. "No problem," Pap reassured me. The family would turn over one of its pigs to me, and I would be responsible for its care. When the pig was big enough, I could sell it and pay off my debt to the family. Although I was not especially enamored with pigs, his proposal seemed reasonable, so I agreed to it.

At first, my relationship to my new acquisition was impersonal. I kept her well fed but otherwise occupied my time with more important matters such as the fate of my beloved Saint Louis Cardinals baseball team. But at some point in her development, for reasons unknown, I reached down and scratched her back while she was eating. She reciprocated her pleasure by grunting. Well, one thing led to another, and before long, when I approached her, she would roll over on her side and expect me to scratch her stomach. In time, I learned exactly how to elicit the most exquisite grunts of satisfaction from her. Alas, in these encounters, I can't remember whether I ever spoke to her or not. Being an Ozarker, I am guessing not.

In any case, Josie, as I named her, soon grew into a substantial-sized hog. I knew she was destined either for sale or breeding, neither of which caused me any concern. What I did not anticipate was a quite different scenario. Pap observed that our large family of six children and two adults needed to butcher another hog and that Josie was the ideal candidate; she was just the right size and age for butchering. By agreeing to this, I would in effect (after paying off my original debt to the family for her) receive the market price for Josie and fulfill my 4-H project obligation as well.

Pap had another idea in mind. He said something like the following: "Ben, you are now a teenager and since you can shoot a .22 rifle accurately, let's have *you* shoot that hog!" I don't remember precisely how I reacted to Pap's suggestion. Perhaps I even welcomed this opportunity to exhibit my maturation into adult responsibilities. In any event, I lowered the family's rifle and shot Josie precisely in the spot I had seen Pap shoot hogs. She buckled. With a sharp butcher knife, Pap at once slit her throat with a knife and blood spurted from the incision.

Later on, when we were cutting Josie up, I blurted out, "I don't want to do that again!" I think Pap said, "I understand." My guess is that despite the killing of animals required by country living, he did not welcome the task. In any case, he never asked me to shoot another hog. After that, my reputation for tenderheartedness was such within the family that my mom never again even asked me to wring the heads of chickens for frying or stewing. Except for annoying insects, I am thinking that I may never have killed another member of the animal kingdom.

23

The Green Beans Were Raw!

My success in transforming Josie into a source of family pork chops, bacon, and hams represented only a small part of my 4-H activities. As one of its main objectives, the 4-H sought to improve the farming and homemaking know-how of its membership, but more important to me were the opportunities that it offered for broadening my cultural horizons and aiding me in overcoming my inherent shyness. For an example of the latter, I remember at a tender age of twelve or so that I had to defend my choices orally to adults when judging vegetables at the Howell County fair. The 4-H also presented me with otherwise unavailable opportunities to develop leadership skills. For at least a couple of terms in my early teens, I served as president of the local club.

Perhaps nothing was quite as controversial during my tenure as my role in organizing and managing a 4-H Sunday.[1] Linking itself to medieval celebrations of God's bounty, 4-H Sunday required club members to attend and to participate in church services on the fifth Sunday after Easter. Seizing on the opportunity to cultivate tolerance of Catholics, despite the fact that I don't think there was a Catholic in the entire Schneider school district, I proposed to our club that we invite members of a 4-H club associated with a German Catholic neighborhood of White Church and Peace Valley (some five miles away) to jointly celebrate with us 4-H Sunday at the local Berean Baptist Church. The program, which featured pledges to the US flag, the Christian flag, and the 4-H flag, among other quasi-liturgical activities, came off without a hitch, though in retrospect, I think witnessing it must have been something of a shock to the parents of the children in both religious groups. In those days in the Ozarks as elsewhere, relations between Catholics and Protestants were none too amicable.

Equally exciting but in a far different way was our local club's participation in a countywide 4-H softball league. Upon learning of this opportunity, my brother Mike, a high school freshman, and I, a sophomore, immediately set about not only strengthening our team via recruitment of at least one key new player—a left-handed first baseman—but also transforming part of the farm's cow pasture into a home playing field. After clearing the field of cow piles, brush, and larger rocks, we laid out a diamond, put up a backstop, and constructed benches for spectators and players. As a fundraising endeavor, we even convinced the girls in the club to sell soda pop at the games.

Of the teams in the league, we had only one formidable foe, the Summers 4-H Club in Howell Valley south of West Plains. The name Summers was appropriate, for most of its players shared that surname. One of them, John Bill, was something of a giant about whom we somehow knew in advance could pound the ball for extraordinarily long distances. Why we didn't simply give him first base by walking him, I do not know, but in the top half of the last inning when we enjoyed a one-run lead, we allowed big John Bill to bat. He clobbered a high drive to left field that appeared to not only be a home run but also to tie the score. Upon retrieval, one of our outfielders (I think it may have been Barbara Hanshaw) threw the ball to me at deep shortstop whereupon I flung the ball to Mike, our catcher who was protecting home plate. Determined to bowl Mike over, big John Bill charged into him. Mike, though at least fifty pounds lighter than Big John, held his ground and the ball. The collision sent Big John sprawling onto his back in agony. We had little sympathy for him, for by this spectacular play, we had won the county 4-H championship!

Another memorable aspect of my engagement in 4-H work revolved around meat judging, which entailed not only making judgments about the relative quality of pieces of beef or whole carcasses but also defending my choices verbally. Although I think my only preparation for the county contest was to read a circular on the subject published by the University of Missouri School of Agriculture, I somehow won the Howell County contest. Bill Rader (not related to my family), the county extension agent responsible for 4-H work, then decided to enter a team comprised of a female 4-Her and me in the state contest in Columbia. Upon my receiving the highest individual score and my teammate third place, much to my surprise, we won the Missouri State 4-H championship in Columbia.

We then competed in the national championship at the American Royal Livestock Show in Kansas City. I quickly began to have doubts about our chances of victory there when I learned that college students majoring in agriculture comprised the other teams. I also remember that the carcasses that we judged in Kansas City were much closer in quality than the ones we had judged in West Plains or Columbia. Our team did perform credibly, but as I recall, we came in thirteenth in the national competition.

As a result of these successes, in 1951 Missouri chose me, a high school junior, to be a delegate to the National 4-H Congress. Beginning with a train ride from Saint Louis to Chicago, nearly everything about the conference was an eye-opening experience. Convening at the skyscraper Hilton Hotel in Chicago, I met and talked to fellow delegates—nearly all students in colleges of agriculture—from the United States as well as several delegates from foreign countries. Apart from speeches, the congress scheduled social events. To this day, I remember the painful experience of a female delegate (doubtless a college student) trying to teach me how to dance. Almost equally memorable was the food served by the hotel. On at least one occasion, the chef served us raw green beans!

24

The Art of Ozarks Bullfighting

Doubtless, few people have ever heard of Ozarks bullfighting. I am unsure how my brother Mike and I got acquainted with the art or lore of the bullring. As I recall, we had only one adult bull on the farm and owned him only briefly. Otherwise, we relied on the services of the bulls of neighbors or the artificial insemination of our cows. Maybe I read about bullfights from Ernest Hemingway or from a more obscure author. Or maybe it had something to do with maleness, with testosterone-driven teenaged boys somehow sensing in testosterone-ridden bulls a worthy foe for teasing.

Even though for the most part, we did not go out of our way to antagonize or challenge the local bulls, I remember that on one occasion we apparently wanted to show off how brave we were to a neighboring boy, Kenneth Coble. So, while we were walking to a Sunday-night church service at the Schneider schoolhouse with Kenneth, we proposed some fun. "Let's tease Dr. Stoll's bull." (Dr. Stoll was an absentee farm owner.) Not spotting the brute at once but bragging of our prowess in tormenting bulls without adverse consequences, we tried calling the Stoll bull or gaining the attention of Stoll's cows but to no avail.

As the sky darkened, we suddenly became aware that Kenneth had disappeared. In our excitement in trying to find Dr. Stoll's bull, neither of us had realized that Kenneth was no longer with us. This was a matter of genuine concern. He did not answer when we repeatedly yelled his name, and we were uncertain that he was familiar with the woods and rough terrain of the Stoll farm. Perhaps he had encountered the bull with disastrous results. For a quarter hour or so, we searched the immediate area for him. Still no Kenneth.

Finally, we continued to the schoolhouse where church services were scheduled. There he was. Our tall talk had petrified him. He had indeed heard us calling, but he was afraid that if he responded to us, the bull would come tumbling out of the woods after him. So he had run as fast as he could back to our house. Pap and Mom had then driven him over to the church services.

Perhaps this should have been the end of our enthusiasm for bullfighting, but it was not. When we acquired about forty head of ewes and an adult ram, or "buck" as we sometimes called him, Mike and I settled on a less dangerous way of developing our skills as toreadors. In a pen, we would taunt the ram by waving a towel or a feed sack at him. The ram could not resist; he charged the towel waver, and at the last moment, the potential victim of his charge would gracefully step aside to avoid the brute's rush. We could then imagine beautiful young swooning Spanish maidens shouting "Olé" and waving their bandanas in acknowledgment of our courage and skill. At the least, our enthusiasm for the bullring suggested that we Ozarkers were not as culturally isolated as many observers believed we were.

Poor Pap was unaware that his eldest sons had been training the old ram for the bullring. So, without concern, one day Pap stepped into the pen to administer a pill to a ewe that would void her of worms. He had turned his back on the ram. The ram charged, *wham*, slamming into Pap's backside at the knees. Pap went down like a sack of potatoes. I don't know about Mike, but as I recall, I had difficulty stifling a laugh. Pap did not think the incident was funny; he grabbed a nearby stick of wood and whacked the ram across the head. The ram shook his head, befuddled. Retaliation was not supposed to be part of the game.

Perhaps needless to add, we never told Pap that we had been training the ram to become a toro bravo.

25

"Mom, We Shot Old Polly!"

When my family purchased the 132-acre farm in Gunter's Valley, it included Pap's vision of having his two oldest sons farm the place while he continued working as an electrician in the nearby town. The year was 1949, and even though tractors had been around for a couple of decades, Pap decided (probably for reasons of economy) that this project would entail farming with horses. So, along with the necessary farm machinery, he bought two mares that we (probably me) named Old Polly and Molly.

No two horses could have been more different. Molly, the younger mare, was flighty and none too bright. Coolheaded and exceptionally smart, Old Polly, on the other hand, seized on every opportunity to take advantage of her counterpart's deficiencies.

To comprehend one way that she did this, consider the following illustration. When two horses are used to pull a plow or a wagon, each animal is harnessed directly to what is called a single tree; the single tree in turn is attached to a double tree; and the double tree is fastened to the tongue of the plow or wagon. For maximum efficiency, each of the horses should be in lockstep with each other as they make their way across the field or down a country road.

Unfortunately, Old Polly recognized right away the possibility of exploiting this situation. When paired to pull a plow or a wagon, she would quickly step out ahead, leaving poor Molly a step behind. This meant that Molly had to do far more than her share of the heavy-duty pulling. Not only that, but sometimes when the force needed to pull a 16 Oliver bottom plow required an equal effort by both horses, Old Polly's tactic brought plowing to an abrupt halt.

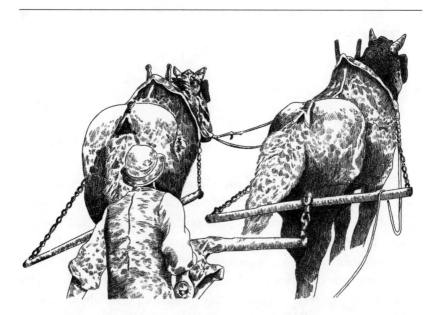

Figure 14. Pulling in unison. In this illustration, the two horses are pulling together, as they should, but imagine a scene in which one of the horses is a step or more out in front of the other. Courtesy of Katie Nieland.

In an effort to even the pulling load of the two mares, my brother or I resorted to whacking Molly across the rump with a whip. Unfortunately, this was not a completely satisfactory solution because poor Molly would then leap ahead of Old Polly. In other words, when plowing a field, instead of observing the team pulling in unison, you might witness the spectacle of the mares seesawing back and forth, one in the lead and then the other. A most unsatisfactory situation.

On one occasion, after a well-delivered lash, Molly leaped forward and slipped on the newly plowed soil. She fell flat on her back. Tangled in her harness and kicking wildly with all four feet, Mike and I were at sea about what to do. Getting close enough to her to unfasten her harness invited the possibility of receiving a smashing blow from one of Molly's flailing hoofs. Finally, we were able to cut away part of her harness and get the horse untangled and upright. Not only was Pap unhappy about this example of our inept management of the mares, but he was also faced with the task of repairing Molly's harness.

Yet another story about the keen intelligence of Old Polly. Of course, both Molly and Old Polly were work rather than saddle horses. Still, Mike and I frequently rode either of the horses bareback if the occasion called for it. One summer, our aunt Pearl Eddings, who was about our age, visited us from Wichita, Kansas. Neither Mike nor I anticipated any problems with having her ride Old Polly. But Old Polly had other ideas. When Aunt Pearl climbed on her back, the old mare immediately wheeled around and tried to bite our aunt on her leg. We reasoned that somehow Old Polly understood that Aunt Pearl was a neophyte when it came to handling horses. So, as with plowing, Old Polly at once sought to take advantage of the situation.

Initially in this farming experiment, my younger brother Mike fared worse—much worse—than me. He was still in grade school and hence after eight months of school was free to toil in April, the month in which we did most of the spring plowing. In the meantime, as a high school freshman, I attended school for nine months and thereby experienced the joys of escaping the spring plowing. Well, mostly. For I was obligated to help plow on Saturdays. But as Grandpa Rader, who was visiting us at the time, observed, "The Lord must be with Ben." For although it remained dry through each week, I think that it rained every Saturday that April!

~

Much to the amusement of Mike and me (and I am sure some people in the neighborhood as well), Pap embarked on another experiment. He bought a young donkey that he hoped would breed one or both of our mares. If the jack were successful, the family would then be the beneficiary of one or more baby mules. I am not quite sure why the jack failed at his assignment. Perhaps the mares were too old. In any event, this is not the end of the story, for the young jack not only loved being around the mares but humans as well. Anytime that we had visitors for Sunday dinners or ball games, for example, he was sure to make an appearance, all too frequently, especially to my mom's utter chagrin, displaying his maleness.

Throughout her life, keeping wise Old Polly fenced in was a problem. While our barbwire fences were not up to even Ozarks standards, they did for the most part contain our cattle and draft animals. But not Old Polly. Somehow, she knew how to unfasten gates or find holes in the fence. In any event, as I remember it, she had an uncanny sense of anticipating when my brother and I were about to engage in some kind of heavy-duty horse work. So, the night before, she, along with Molly and the jack, would sneak off from the farm, always heading north. Hence, Mike and I spent at least half of the next day tracking down the elusive animals. In doing so, our neighbors aided us. After all, who could forget seeing two mares followed by a jack trotting down a country road?

~

Old Polly repeatedly breached the fence surrounding our house and garden as well. Once inside, she headed for Mom's garden and began feasting on the luscious vegetables that Mom had spent countless hours nursing. I suppose that Pap from time to time tried to repair the fence and devise gates that he hoped would keep Old Polly at bay but to no avail.

One Sunday afternoon, while Mom was working in the kitchen, she heard the boom of a shotgun blast. Moments later, my four-year-old sister, Ada, burst into the kitchen and proudly announced, "Mom, we shot Old

Polly!" Utterly stunned, Mom thought that Pap had killed the old mare. Pap tried to reassure her that he had no intention of killing Old Polly, that he had only fired nonlethal (but painful) buckshot into her rump. This, he explained (or perhaps more accurately, hoped), would deter her from coming into the yard and eating our garden in the future. Mom was not fully mollified. "Shooting Old Polly in the presence of your young daughter certainly does not set a very good example," she said.

However, Mom loved to tell this story—and with a smile. If not at once, she in time found her husband's characteristically Ozarker solution to the problem, along with her young daughter's response to the shooting, both imaginative and funny.

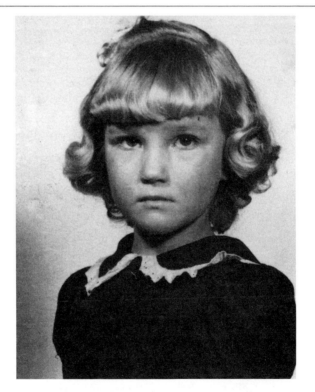

Figure 15. School photo of my sister Ada when she was a six-year-old. As Ada observed in a recent email to me, looking at this photo suggests that she was not all that thrilled about shooting Old Polly. Courtesy of the author.

26

The Failure of the Great Multiflora Rose Experiment

I'll not name names, but an Ozarker I know well phoned to congratulate me on the publication of my book, *Down on Mahans Creek: A History of an Ozarks Neighborhood* (2017). "I love your book," he explained. "I stayed up most of last night to finish reading it." To impress me with how much he liked the book and the momentous nature of his feat, he added that my book was only the second one that he had completed reading in his entire lifetime of seventy-plus years.

I then dutifully responded, "What was the other book that you read?" "The Bible," he retorted. Now, I can hardly deny taking pride in learning that *Down on Mahans Creek* had joined such distinguished company, but it occurred to me that this incident might be a starting point for considering the intellectual life of the Ozarks.

As perhaps with no other region in the country, there is and always has been a substantial portion of its residents that looks down on what they might describe as "book learnin.'" To them, in terms of utility, common or horse sense nearly always trumped the formal knowledge propounded by educators. Put another way, one is better off relying on folk wisdom than turning to books or teachers for solutions to the pressing problems that routinely plague human existence.

While doing research on the Mahans Creek neighborhood, I found plenty of hard evidence, at least in the early years of the twentieth century, to support this contention. Less than half of children of an appropriate age regularly showed up for school in Delaware. Of these, boys attended far less frequently than girls. "They came to school only when they felt inclined," reported one of my great-uncles, Elva Pummill, a one-room rural school-master in a nearby township.[2] Families of modest means, I speculated, needed the income generated by their school-aged boys and reasoned that work experience might reward their futures more than formal learning.

Still, there were exceptions. Take my grandpa Rader, for example. Born in 1874 and attending primary school only sporadically, Grandpa himself took great pride in his spelling and handwriting skills. In the spelling exercises of his day, the student first pronounced the entire word, then pronounced and spelled each syllable separately, and finally pronounced the entire word again. He liked to regale his children and, later on, his grandchildren with his rendition of spelling the word "incomprehensibility." I am uncertain at what age I learned to spell this word, but wishing to avoid embarrassment by his repeated queries, I soon learned. He regularly put his grandchildren to spelling tests. How do you spell "gnat," he once asked Carl Herren, one of his exceptionally bright grandchildren. After careful deliberation, Carl responded, "K-n-a-t." "He had fooled me and was tickled about it," remembered Carl.[3]

Then there was the maternal side of my father's family, the Pummills. Although they loved the dilatory life in the hollows, including hunting and fishing, they were different. Unlike most of their neighbors, who themselves or their ancestors came from the heartland of the Upland South (especially Tennessee and Kentucky), their paternal side migrated to Shannon County via the region's periphery (southern Ohio and central Missouri), and the maternal side (the Matthews family) featured an array of preachers and teachers. They relished book learning, reciting poetry, and engaging in oratory. They aspired, as one of them put it, "to do great things." Of the John Pummill–Lydia Matthews children, six of the seven at one time or another taught school.

~

At some point, I may have become an unwitting convert to the Pummill side of Ozarks intellectual life. Maybe it was when I became the unofficial reporter of World War II for the Delaware School. Looking back after all these years, I must concede with some reluctance that I was an arrogant child; perhaps my displays of arrogance stemmed from attempts to disguise my personal insecurities. I remember a fellow student at lunchtime at Delaware once asking me, "Is your big head the reason that you are so smart?" However, I was even better known by the prominence of my ears, which stuck straight out from my head, though I doubt if either of these peculiar physical characteristics had much to do with my developing adherence to the book learning tradition.

In any case, attendance at a one-room rural school reinforced rather than dampened my interest in books. Given that the teacher was most of the time occupied with instructing other students, I was free to read whatever I could get my hands on. This meant reading *everything* in the school library, which consisted of two kinds of books—popular, romantic novels published early in the twentieth century and government publications, especially those pertaining to agriculture, which, I think, the school library had obtained for free.

The latter, I took seriously. Wading through the bulletins of the University of Missouri Agricultural Experimental Station published in Columbia and the massive yearbooks of the United States Department of Agriculture published in Washington, DC, I came to a startling conclusion. I discovered that the ways that Pap farmed were archaic. Rather than resting on the latest scientific research, I reasoned, they sprang from irrational folk practices passed down to him by previous generations.

So I became something of an evangelist within the family for the most recent findings of the agricultural experts. I urged the use of more fertilizers and hybrid seeds, the planting of the latest pasture crops, and (rather than scrubs) the ownership of pedigree cattle and hogs. Despite our modest financial resources, to a surprising degree Pap bought into my recommendations. At least I thought that he did, but his acquiescence to my recommendations might have been part of a strategy to keep me on the farm.

I now acknowledge in my senior dotage that more often than not, I was wrong, that in the end, the folk wisdom of the Ozarks usually rewarded the local farmers more than the latest book learning emanating out of Columbia, Missouri or Washington, DC. Indeed, much of the advice of the experts rested on experimentation on lands quite different from the Ozarks and on the premise that the farmers had lots of money to invest.

Suffice it for me to offer one vivid example. In the 1940s, the Missouri State Soil Conservation Service nursery pioneered in experimenting with the multiflora rose, a plant native to Japan, as a living fence and wild animal habitat. By the 1950s, the Missouri Conservation Commission was distributing at cost to farmers enough multiflora rose plants to construct one thousand miles of fence annually. Inedible for domesticated farm animals, the thorny plant spread across Missouri (as well as other rural areas of

America) with astonishing rapidity, gobbling up acre after acre of pasture and field cropland as it went.

Extraordinarily difficult to eradicate, it was not until 1983 that the Missouri Conservation service finally declared it a "noxious weed." The service reluctantly, it seemed, conceded the monumental failure of their experiment with these words: "This plant has taught land managers a hard lesson about hindsight."[4] I am not quite sure how the service had the gall to transfer the blame for this experiment from themselves to the "land managers"—that is, to the farmers themselves—but as you can see, they did.

Be that as it may, in time, Pap became an implacable enemy of multiflora rose. Every time that he drove his pickup truck out over his acreage, he carried with him an axe and a hoe. He attacked both multiflora rose plants and Canadian thistles with equal ardor.

A self-damning conclusion follows. As with the disastrous consequences of the multiflora rose experiment, Pap would have been better off in the long run had he ignored most of the badgering of his son on behalf of "book learnin'" agriculture. I now seize on this occasion to concede that Pap (nearly) always knew what was best.

The following vignette examines hunting as an important male activity in the Ozarks.

27

When Mom Awoke to the Roar of a Chain Saw

Mom awoke to the roar of a chain saw ripping through the night's silence. She reached across the bed to alert Pap. Pap was not there! Puzzled and concerned, she continued listening. The chain saw suddenly stopped, and then faintly, as if in the distance, she heard a tree crashing down and dogs barking. She then put the puzzle together. Now an old man, Pap was out in the woods alone in the middle of the night. He had cut down a tree so that his young hounds could fight the coon that came tumbling out of its branches.

~

Pap came from a coon-hunting family. Whether his grandfather, George Washington Rader, was a coon hunter is unknown, but family lore does accord a special place to one of his distant ancestors back in "Old Kentuck" who fell over a bluff while coon hunting. The accident left Uncle Bartley without the full powers of speech and so facially disfigured that the children in the neighborhood were afraid of him. When the children misbehaved, their mothers threatened to sic Uncle Bartley onto them. Maybe his face was the reason that Uncle Bartley never married.

A shared enthusiasm for hunting had far-reaching consequences for the Rader-Pummill clan in the Mahans Creek neighborhood. It helped to knit the dilatory Raders to a far more ambitious family—the Pummills—who settled on the creek in the 1890s. When the Pummills arrived, according to one report, "the streams were teeming with fish and the woods were full of wild game such as deer, fox, turkey." Indeed, no omen of the Pummill family's future on the creek was more auspicious than the early hunting success of Arthur Pummill. As a twelve-year-old lad, a few days before Christmas in 1892, Arthur set out before dawn to hunt with his brother-in-law Jim Rader. "They caught a possum, a coon and a squirrel."[5]

In 1929, as an adult, Arthur organized the Shannon County Foxhunters Association. A crowd of some five hundred hunters from several Ozarks counties plus more than a hundred hounds camped out in October near his farm for a weekend of competitive hunting. The first night, Arthur scheduled "three good races"; the second night, he set up a medley of races, trials, speeches, and a fiddle-playing contest. That night, "a clamor went up for a dancing floor." Arthur built one the next day, and that day, the frivolities continued far into the night. "There was plenty of everything as advertised," the local *Current Wave* newspaper observed, "and a little more of a certain article, however no particular unpleasantness was reported."[6] Although none may have equaled the excitement of the 1929 meet, the county's foxhunters continued to hold annual competitions through the next two decades.

One of Arthur's sons, Dave—Pap's closest friend as a young man—became Shannon County's most renowned woodsman. By the time of his death at the age of ninety in 1997, no single person in the county knew the hills, hollers, and crannies of the county better than Dave. As a young man, such was his local reputation as a hunter that someone nicknamed him Crockett. The name was so appropriate that it stuck for his entire lifetime.

~

Describing himself to his kinfolk as a "backwoodsman" and a "lover of women," Grandpa Sam Rader himself was no slouch as a hunter, especially when it came to hunting coons. He doted on his hounds; he baked them corn bread and fed them watermelon rinds. His favorite hound was Caruso, named for the famed Italian operatic tenor whom he had heard sing on the family's hand-cranked Victrola. That he named the dog Caruso, I like to point out, suggests that the residents of this isolated spot in the Ozarks were not nearly as out of touch with the outside world or modernity as many observers believe them to have been.

As I mentioned, Sam loved women, perhaps as much as coonhounds. Unfortunately, his beloved dark-haired wife, Ada Mae Pummill, died in 1912, leaving him with alone with six children. He sank into a deep "melancholia," but after an appropriate time of mourning, he began to look for a replacement. He learned of a winsome widow living in the nearby town of Winona. The courtship went smoothly. Sam owned a reasonably good farm on Mahans Creek, and the widow even liked Sam's rambunctious children. But when Sam proposed marriage, she made an unexpected demand: Sam had to choose either her or his hounds—a painful choice. Sam chose his hounds.

Until the very end, Grandpa Sam loved hunting. In 1950, at the age of seventy-six, before dawn, he rode out alone with his hounds to coon hunt. While slowly picking his way down an exceptionally steep ridge, Old Rock, his normally reliable saddle horse stumbled, throwing him to the ground and breaking his hip. Old Rock proceeded home without him. Despite excruciating pain, Grandpa Sam somehow managed to blow his cow horn. Hearing its lonely wail far down the creek, Hulbert, one of his sons, eventually found him. Grandpa never fully recovered. He died from a heart attack not long afterward, but he would be the first to say that he would prefer to die in no other way than by hunting.

~

Neither did Grandpa's death dissuade Pap from continuing to coon hunt. He had for a number of years a prized hound that he named Old Moses. This was because the story of the dog's very existence paralleled that of the biblical story of how the pharaoh's daughter saved the life of the infant Moses by rescuing him from the bulrushes along the river Nile. With enough hounds already at his disposal, Pap had decided to slay the unwanted pups of the mother of Old Moses, which he proceeded to do, with one exception. After having killed the pups, he later happened to notice a live pup in the weeds alongside one of the ponds that he had missed killing. Recalling the legend of Moses, he decided to let the pup live and named him Moses.

Alas, for the most part, unlike Grandpa, Pap treated his hounds poorly. Had it not been for Mom, they would have frequently gone hungry, and she did not even particularly like hounds. Pap's neglect of Old Moses apparently prompted the hound to run off with startling frequency. Pap then had to set out searching for him. On occasion, Old Moses simply disappeared for days at a time. But eventually, Pap heard about his whereabouts, perhaps many miles away, and retrieved him from a family who presumably took better care of him.

I never heard Pap say it was so, but he must have been disappointed with the utter absence of any interest in hunting by his two oldest sons. Only on rare occasions did either Mike or I agree to go out in the middle of night and coon hunt with him. Neither did we engage in other kinds of hunting or do much fishing. The hunting gene apparently skipped a generation.

But as fortune would have it, the next generation was entirely a different matter. Entering his final years, Pap frequently went coon hunting with one of his grandsons, Lance Cochran. And by far the champion hunter of his direct descendants is Lance's son, Mason Cochran, who as a high school student, accompanied by his girlfriend, took it upon himself to keep the deer population of Howell County, Missouri healthy by systematically thinning its population.

~

On a more serious note, there are no more powerful icons of Ozarks uniqueness than the twin *H*'s, hunting and hounds. By way of a juxtaposition, think, for example, of the arcadia of the ancient Greeks. If American painter Thomas Cole is correct, the Greek arcadia is a pastoral one, a rural scene of open meadows occupied by shepherds with their dogs tending their flocks. In the meadow's foreground is also a diaphanously clad woman and in the background a religious shrine. To represent the arcadia of the Ozarks, on the other hand, requires a painting of deep woods, narrow, steep hollers, one or more hound(s), and a lone hunter. No partly nude women or spired churches here. As far as I know, the Ozarks are still awaiting a modern Thomas Cole to do the region full justice.

28

How Clarence Renfro Failed to Make His Case

After building themselves a primitive shelter, no bigger problem confronted the first settlers in the Ozarks than figuring out how to protect their crops and gardens from would-be marauders. One tactic that Pap employed to keep insects and worms from eating our garden was to grow a small crop of tobacco. He then harvested the tobacco not only for his own use—to make his own cigarettes, to fire up his corncob pipe, or to chew—but also to spit the juice onto garden plants. The unsavory juice, it was believed, dissuaded bugs and cutworms from eating your vegetable plants.

Crows as well as rabbits and coons could also do serious damage to crops. Apart from trying to shoot them, farmers might seek to frighten them away by posting lifelike scarecrows in their fields. Be assured that none of these measures was foolproof. Then there were the wild dogs that roamed the neighborhood. On one occasion, they killed several of my sheep before I could ward them off with our old .22 rifle.

Alas, these enemies were not the only ones. Lurking in the nearby woods were even more serious would-be intruders—cattle, horses, and above all, hogs. Hogs were especially adept at not only surviving in the woods but also reproducing themselves quickly and, in short order, destroying a farmer's crops. They not only ate the plants but uprooted them as well. No ordinary fence could keep them out of your cornfield or your vegetable garden. But, of course, the early setters had no woven wire, no metal fence posts, no way of stretching a fence tightly, and rarely much money.

They did have other resources. They may have owned or could borrow an axe, perhaps a wedge or two, and maybe a saw. And nearby, there were trees, frequently lots of them. So the new settlers early on embarked on the backbreaking job of building a rail fence around the plot in which they planned to plant corn or vegetables. A white oak rail fence might, with regular repairs and replacements, last up to twenty years. Cedar was even sturdier, but there was not much of it around. Splitting the rails was not for everyone. It required muscular power and precision, skills that made Abraham Lincoln and Paul Bunyan folk heroes. Not quite as skilled as these folk heroes, I presume, Grandpa Raz Eddings once cut off three of his toes while splitting rails as a young man. Incidentally, Raz buried the toes. He did not want dogs or hogs eating them.

Apart from rotting, periodic flooding and forest fires could do untold damage to rail fences. In my own family history, a fire in 1887 in the Mahans Creek neighborhood destroyed over a thousand rails on the J. Ben Searcy farm. The possibility of devastating forest fires increased with the newly arrived railroad into the neighborhood in the 1890s. Sparks from the locomotives set off brush fires that could in turn set rail fences afire. But even more significant were the huge neighborhood floods in 1892 and 1895. Apart from lifting the Delaware schoolhouse from its foundations and carrying it some sixty yards downstream where it lodged up against some trees, the great flood of 1895 washed away newly planted corn crops and mile after mile of rail fencing. For several days, a stench hung over the hollow.

In time, Ozarks farmers replaced rail fences with woven and barbwire, but fencing remained a major problem. Fence construction required regular maintenance and money that the farmers frequently did not have. And there remained the renegade farm animals that managed to damage or break through fencing. Farmers routinely had to replace rotted posts and gates.

One of the ever-present problems on Mahans Creek was to maintain a satisfactory fence across the creek itself. Since fence posts could not be driven into the loose sand in the bottom of the creek, farmers tried to devise some kind of "water gap," a special fence across the creek that would allow for the continuous flow of water while simultaneously keeping animals in or out. None of these seemed to work well; high water from heavy rainfalls was particularly a problem. Hay, leaves, brush, limbs, even substantial-sized logs frequently jammed up against the gap and eventually would break through it.

A downpour in about 1950 in Howell County washed out the gap between our farm and that of a neighbor, Bob Stevenson. Not only that but our cows—perhaps lured by Bob's bull—had managed to make their way through the ruptured fence onto the Stevenson farm. The morning after, when we discovered this situation, Pap explained that he had to go to work in town. He ordered me not only to recover and milk the cows but also to repair the water gap. Not especially enthusiastic about attending high school classes that day, I offered no opposition to this plan.

But the next day, in order to be readmitted to classes, I had to confront Clarence Renfro, West Plains High School's formidable principal. I did not expect any difficulties in obtaining an excused absence; after all, I had been ordered by Pap to skip school. But Mr. Renfro put me on the spot. He posed this question: "Why didn't your dad fix the water gap?" I responded, "But he had to go to work." Then Mr. Renfro said, much to my surprise, "Tell your dad that you attending school is more important than his going to work." Of course, I was delighted to relay Mr. Renfro's response to Pap.

At the time, I think I agreed with the esteemed principal's position, but in retrospect, I am not so sure that Clarence Renfro made his case. Jeopardizing our family of six children's income was surely a more serious matter than me missing a day of school. Besides, I expect that once I had retrieved the cows, the jackass, and the mares, milked the cows, and fixed

Figure 16. Ben Rader, West Plains, Missouri high school graduation class photo, 1953. Courtesy of the author.

the water gap that I spent the remainder of the day reading a book. Maybe I learned more from the book than I would have by attending classes.

29

And Barbara Said That He Looked Like Mickey Mantle

You may have an idyllic picture of living down on the farm. From *Saturday Evening Post* lithographs, watching *Green Acres* on television, or reading bucolic novels, you may imagine a farm featuring a white, two-story, framed house surrounded by an equally white picket fence. Inside the yard, you would see a couple of children chasing a ball. Nearby is a red barn with a haymow on the second floor and stalls for horses and cattle on the first floor. In the wintertime, adolescent boys might play basketball on the second floor and young people sometimes gathered there for parties or barn dances. Near the barn, you might imagine contented cows chewing their cuds, colts frisking about, and a hound dog sniffing out a rabbit in the lilac bushes.

Although there is much to commend this Edenic setting, in my experience of the Ozarks, this picture frequently fell short of reality. We never had a picket fence around our yard; indeed, we had no yard fence on Mahans Creek or on our first farm near West Plains. Few of our neighbors had them either. Until I read *The Adventures of Tom Sawyer*, I didn't even know what a picket fence was. Rather than a picket fence, neatly trimmed shrubs, or a closely mowed lawn, near the typical Ozarker house, one was more likely to find a shade tree or two, uncut weeds, a dilapidated outhouse, and parts of old cars or rusting farm machinery littered about.

Neither did Ozarkers for the most part have painted barns, let alone red ones. Barn siding nearly always consisted of cheap, unpainted, weather-beaten oak boards. Over the years, the barns took on strange shapes, rusted, corrugated tin roofs slanted in unexpected directions, and the structures leaned precariously in one direction or the other. Indeed, to keep them from falling over, farmers sometimes had to prop them up with two-by-fours or oak poles. And rather than a quiet and peaceful scene, a cacophony of bawling calves, squealing pigs, crowing roosters, neighing horses, and barking dogs all greeted you or disturbed your serenity.

But I can think of nothing that more flatly contradicts the idyllic rendering of farms than the prevalence of squishy, stinky cow piles. On dairy farms in particular, it was virtually impossible to navigate one's way around barnyards or in the barns themselves without stepping on a cow pile, or what some of the more daring farmers described as cow s**t. Those who prefer euphemisms called them cow piles, cow pies, or cow manure. On the plus side, by spreading it out over your garden or your cornfield, cow manure can improve your yields. Still, no task on the farm is more unpleasant than this one.

~

There was no ready market for fresh milk down on Mahans Creek, but Pap soon learned that West Plains had a cheese factory and that milking Jersey cows (preferred because of their milk's high butterfat content) was common among the farmers in the area in which we lived. So when we moved over to the larger farm in Gunter's Valley, he bought a few milk cows, and he expected that Mike and I would milk them twice daily, once before we made off to high school and again late in the afternoon after we had returned from school. Each morning, on his way to work, Pap himself delivered the milk to the cheese factory.

Unlike the milk that you pour into your breakfast cereal each morning (which is produced in superclean quarters and is pasteurized), the cheese factory imposed virtually no cleanliness standards on the dairy farmers. Our only concession to cleanliness was to gently wash the cow's udder and teats—a procedure that we did not always follow—and to strain the milk through a cheesecloth, which did remove the drowned flies and the feces that the cow's tail might have flung into the pail while she was being milked.

There are little known secrets about how to milk a cow successfully. Since cows can be anxious animals, they have to be induced to "let down" their milk. Simply feeding them will not normally do the trick. You must treat them with respect. This means taking a teat in each hand and alternating hands as you gently pull down on the teat. They also like to be spoken to in a soothing, modulated voice and to have you, while milking, lean your head gently into the side of their belly. The result of your ministrations should be not only seeing the milk pour into the bucket but also filling the air with the scent of sweet, warm milk. If you own a barn cat, they will quickly appear on the scene, begging you to squirt a teat full of milk into their open mouths.

But I digress. Keeping your clothes reasonably clean in a dairy barnyard was no easy task. Since it was virtually impossible to keep cow excrement off your shoes, the only safe procedure was to wear overshoes or have a separate pair of shoes for milking. To change both shoes and pants for milking twice a day seemed to me particularly burdensome. So at times, I changed only my shoes. But alas, this slovenly practice sometimes caught up with me.

On occasion, when in my literature class sitting next to the prettiest town girl—one whom I wanted to impress mightily—the waft of cow manure drifted up from the cuffs of my blue jeans. It was little wonder that in such a situation, I was tongue-tied. My brother Mike, on the other hand, not only always changed his shoes—indeed, he might even take the extra precaution of shining them—but also changed his blue jeans after milking. Maybe it was for that reason that he enjoyed more success with the girls than I did, though there could have been other reasons as well. After all, my wife, Barbara, many years later said that Mike looked like Mickey Mantle. Maybe he did, but even if so, Barbara's observation did not offer me much comfort.

Figure 17. My year-younger brother E. M. "Mike" Rader, as a West Plains, Missouri, high school junior, 1953. While growing up in the Ozarks, we were exceptionally close companions and sometimes antagonists. Courtesy of the author.

30

"Thank You, Mr. Fernetti"

There was a time in which you could live your entire life without coming across somebody with an Italian surname. At least this was the case down in the part of the Ozarks where I came from. Lots of Smiths, Johnsons, Campbells, Williamses, and the like whose ancestors were from the British Isles as well as even a few scattered German last names, but rarely indeed did one encounter a Rizzo, Esposito, De Luca, or Colombo, let alone a Fernetti.

But this is precisely what happened to me when I walked into my high school junior English class in West Plains, Missouri in 1951. There, in the front of the room next to his desk stood a bona fide Italian American, tall, dark, and handsome.

"I am Mr. Fernetti, your English teacher," he announced.

Neither my classmates nor I expected this. Not only did he look different, but he was a *man* teaching English! And as far as we knew, only women possessed the requisite qualities for converting Ozarks teenagers from the language they had learned at their mother's knee to a wholly new set of alien rules said to be the King's English. Only women could get excited about verb tenses, outlining sentences, or spending time on figures of speech. Perhaps as latter-day Victorians, we also thought it a woman's job to preserve and promote the nation's literary heritage.

In any case, men taught *manly* courses: driver's education, biology, vocational agriculture, and shop. Above all else, men coached: football, basketball, and track. And as if that was not enough, they taught boys physical education or even on occasion history, though a man teaching history was considered somewhat suspect.

Still, I think that we may have cut Mr. Fernetti some slack, for he was newly married to a gorgeous blonde, who also began her teaching career in English at West Plains High School in 1951. To the boys at least, she was just about as unusual as him being an Italian and teaching English.

Aldon Fernetti shattered our preconceived notions about a lot of things. He was not only the first Italian American we had ever encountered, but he

Figure 18. Aldon Fernetti, teacher of senior English and literature at West Plains High School, 1953. Courtesy of the author.

also came from a coal-mining family in the Pittsburg, Kansas area. Before entry into World War II, he himself had toiled in the coal mines. Soon, we learned that coal miners belonged to *labor unions* and on occasion even went on strike for higher wages and better working conditions. It was not long before we recognized that he held strange views on the political issues of the day as well. In class discussions, he quietly but (in my opinion) persuasively made the case for General Dwight Eisenhower over Senator Robert Taft for the Republican presidential nomination in 1952. But it was not long before I sensed that his true passion was not Ike but somebody else, Adlai Stevenson, the Democratic nominee in 1952 who was known for the quality of his mind and his skill with words. (A substantial majority of the West Plains High School students were Republicans.)

Even more shocking, Mr. Fernetti challenged our preconceptions of race. He required the class to read a little essay (alas, I have forgotten the title and the author) from *Reader's Digest*. In the subsequent discussion, he asked the class something like, "What do you think about Negroes?" Although most of us were too stunned to volunteer a response, one student observed that he did not like them. "Why?" asked Mr. Fernetti. "Because, they smell," he said. From there, the discussion proceeded with an exploration of racial stereotypes.

But it was not only his personal qualities or challenges to our preconceptions of labor unions, politics, or race that struck me and some (probably a minority) of my classmates so forcefully. It was his unwavering enthusiasm for the life of the mind. He loved ideas. Never before had my classmates or I met anyone so enamored with reading and literature. He revealed to us the brilliance of Shakespeare, the poetry of Walt Whitman, and the vernacular of Mark Twain. At least a few of us joined in his love fest.

Thank you, Mr. Fernetti!

Although we never met face-to-face after my senior course in literature with him in 1951–52, I did—too many years later—express my gratitude to him in a personal letter. After earning a master's degree in literature from Pittsburg State College (Kansas) and teaching for several decades at Shawnee Mission North High School in Kansas, Aldon Fernetti passed away from cancer in 2003.

31

"I'm from Missouri, and You Have Got to Show Me"

I imagine that most people dismiss the Missouri motto of "The Show Me State" as a bunch of hokum that Missourians, especially those from the Ozarks, employ to camouflage their general ignorance or to enhance their otherwise weak self-esteem. This may be so, but the intrinsic skepticism said to be characteristic of Missourians extends back to the nineteenth century. As early as 1899, Congressman Willard Duncan Vandiver, a former science teacher, declared on the floor of the US Congress, "I come from a state that raises corn and cotton, cockleburs and Democrats, and frothy eloquence neither convinced nor satisfies me. I am from Missouri, and you have got to show me."

How many Missourians share Congressman Vandiver's view is unknown, but from my firsthand experience, I think many Ozarkers take pride in embracing the motto, at least to the extent of possessing a hardheaded skepticism toward the more outlandish claims of others. This seems to have been the case with several members of my family.

In the instance of my maternal grandfather, Alford "Raz" Eddings, the show-me spirit applied to just about everything that defied common sense. This meant that he rejected the idea that the earth was round and that we lived in a heliocentric universe. He once shocked me by completely denying the moon landing, even though he had observed it on television. He believed it was a hoax perpetuated by the Democrats to win votes!

Perhaps strangely enough, however, he accepted uncritically a large body of folk medical cures. Once, when our baby son developed an earache, he told my wife, Barbara, that we should take down the shotgun and kill a rabbit. Then we should press the warm innards of the rabbit against the infected ear. (This was yet another reminder to Barbara that she had married into a strange culture.) Indeed, Raz fancied himself as something of a medicine man. Said to have had Native American ancestry, he collected roots and herbs from the hills and hollows around Ink, Missouri and administered them to sick neighbors and members of his own family.

Raz's belief system could be funny if infuriating. After he had retired as an electrician, Pap volunteered to help Raz build a new home on a few acres outside of Neodesha, Kansas. Pap at once ran into difficulties with Raz; for example, Raz initially refused to pour the cement for the foundation of the new house because, as he explained, it was in the wrong phase of the moon. Hence, Pap, who was anxious to get back to his own home in the Ozarks, had to wait for the right phase of the moon before they could proceed.

But this was not the end of his problems with Raz's beliefs. When Pap began to install electrical outlets in the new structure at the standard height of twelve to sixteen inches from the floor, Raz objected. He insisted that

Figure 19. Grandpa Alford Eddings and Lowell "Pap" Rader in about 1970. Courtesy of the author.

they be four feet (forty-eight inches) from the floor. At first, Pap resisted, observing that this was a highly unorthodox place to put outlets. But when Raz responded that outlets at four feet made it a lot easier for older folk such as Grandma and himself to plug in and unplug vacuum cleaners and the like, Pap had to concede that in this case, Raz's logic was beyond question.

~

I confess that the religious skepticism frequently found in the (male-only) Rader side of my family had roots back in Kentucky, not in Missouri. The first Rader, one Karl Rader, born in Germany, apparently resisted the blandishments of the local evangelicals in Hart County, Kentucky. So did a long line of his male descendants who later settled in the Ozarks. The males nearly always conformed to the following narrative.

Initially, they had little to do with organized religion, despite the pervasive religiosity found in their neighborhoods. Presumably, for them, the claims of organized religion did not pass the show-me test. But as they became old men and approached death, they, like the French thinker Blaise Pascal, decided not to take any chances. They then confessed their sins and their belief in God and agreed to be baptized into (usually) a Baptist or sometimes a Methodist church.

32

"I Must Go to the Eleanor"

There was a time when just about everybody who lived in the countryside had either a Chick Sale or an Eleanor. If you don't know what these terms refer to, you can be forgiven. Few people do. A hint: A Chick Sale has nothing to do with the sale of baby chicks or to young women whose dalliances are up for auction. Neither does an Eleanor. Both terms are euphemisms for outdoor toilets!

The first usage of the term "Chick Sale" that I encountered was by one of my great-aunts, Crystal Pummill, the wife of a mathematics professor at the normal school (teacher's college) in Springfield, Missouri. Crystal observed in a memoir that when the Pummills decided to establish a campground on their farm down on Mahans Creek in 1932, they cleared the grounds of underbrush, erected a rail fence around the plot, and built "an excellent cabin" as well as "a two holer *Chick Sales*" in the back. No isolated Ozarker was she.

The truth is that these euphemisms owe their existence to the Republican Party and to a rail-thin stand-up vaudevillian from Urbana, Illinois, one Charles "Chic" Sale. In 1929, Sale began performing a comedic act about an outhouse builder named Lem Putt. Adept at mimicking a rural accent,

Sale's monologue caught on at once. He published its contents in a little book titled, *The Specialist*, which went through several editions. It became so popular that it even incurred the envy of novelist William Faulkner. By the way, Sale came to resent the renaming of outhouses after him. Why not call them Lem Putts? he queried.

As you might expect, scholars have subsequently proposed several highfalutin ideas to explain the popularity of Sale's book. Remember that despite the Roaring Twenties of F. Scott Fitzgerald and his wife, Zelda, in the 1930s many Americans had still not gotten over the Victorian age, a time in which people routinely employed euphemisms when speaking about human body parts and functions, provided that they spoke about them at all. Hence, Sale, while making the outdoor toilet the subject of his act and his book, not only broke with this taboo but also titillated his uptight audiences by offering suggestive details of what went on inside an outhouse. For example, he observed that younger people preferred using the pages of Sears and Roebuck catalogs while oldsters opted for corncobs. As part of the fun, he did not explicitly explain the purpose of either. He left that to the listener's or reader's imagination.

In any event, Chic Sale contributed mightily to transforming the outhouse into one of the quintessential icons that constituted what it meant to be a hillbilly. By the mid-1930s, when one thought of the hillbillies living in Appalachia or the Ozarks, they conjured up images of log cabins, moonshine, hound dogs, feuds, and of course, outhouses. For many years, this iconography remained unchanged. Consider one of the most popular television shows in the nation's history, *The Beverly Hillbillies* (1962–71). When the Clampett family struck it rich and traded living in the Ozarks for life in sunny Southern California, they loaded up their outhouse in the back of their old jalopy and brought it with them. In sum, it seems plausible to argue that a Chic Sale, along with the other Ozarks icons, functioned for many Americans as something of a psychic sanctuary from the hustle and bustle of modern life.

All of this of course had little to do with the realities of those who made regular use of outdoor toilets. For Ozarkers, in terms of the hierarchy of farm architecture, the outdoor privy stood at or very near the bottom—well below your house, barn, toolshed, or even your chicken house. I remember that its very existence was something of an embarrassment. Hastily built with cheap green oak lumber that soon turned gray with age, standing atop earthen pits, and ventilated by spaces between the boards or sometimes a quarter moon–shaped hole in the door, Ozarks' farmers tried to put them out of the sight of visitors. And to state it bluntly, they stank, and as often as not, users had to contend with flies and sometimes wasps and snakes. Its maintenance was simple; once the pit below the seats had filled with human offal, you simply dug another hole nearby and moved the toilet on top of it. The typical outhouse was a "two-holer"—a larger hole for the bigger folks and a smaller hole for the tots. As you might expect, outhouses were tempting targets for Halloween pranksters.

Not all outhouses occupied such an inferior status. Far from it. To put the unemployed to work, improve the standards of hygiene, and prevent contagious diseases, Franklin D. Roosevelt's New Deal in the 1930s embarked on a massive project that resulted in the construction of 2.3 million new outdoor toilets. Well over half of them went to individual families who paid for the building materials but not the labor, while the other half resulted in new outhouses for schools, churches, and public parks. The design of the New Deal "sanitary units" improved on the traditional outhouse. The New Deal version included concrete floors, a concrete vault to hold the offal, and a superior ventilation system. By visiting your local city park, you can sometimes find surviving examples of this form of New Deal architecture.

That the president's wife, Eleanor, was an enthusiastic proponent of this program led the Republicans to lampoon the New Deal outhouses as "Eleanors." I guess they didn't get much mileage from this uncharitable designation, since FDR won reelection three times. Besides, do you ever remember anyone saying, "I must go to the Eleanor"?

The following vignette treats a key transition in my life—from rural to urban, from high school to college, and from farming to working in a gigantic factory (Boeing Aircraft Company).

33

A Day in the Life of a Jig Builder

Upon my graduation from high school in the spring of 1953, my brother Mike (having finished his junior year in high school) and I boarded a Trailways bus in West Plains. After several exchanges, we arrived about ten hours later in Wichita, Kansas, some four hundred miles away. We then moved into the basement of Grandpa and Grandma Eddings's small, white bungalow on Hydraulic Street. Jobs were plentiful in Wichita; only a few days later, I began to work full time for the Royal Crown Cola Bottling Company and Mike did likewise for a local grocery store. Little did we comprehend that we were part of a great mid-twentieth-century Ozarks diaspora or that living in Wichita for a few years would "case-harden" our future lives.[7]

To comprehend the momentous importance of this move to us, consider our previous work experience. Even though it was in the 1950s, our work ways in striking respects resembled those of our nineteenth-century ancestors. We planted and harvested corn and put up hay with horses, not tractors. The seasons, the daylight hours, and the weather rather than the clock or machines dictated the pace of our work. During planting and harvesting seasons, we necessarily toiled harder, sometimes laboring from daybreak to dark. Even in wintertime, cattle, pigs, and sheep had to be fed, fences repaired, and cows milked. But otherwise, there were long lulls in work, even in the summertime. During these downtimes, we frequently practiced softball, baseball, or basketball. Or I might read a book or a magazine. Daily life then was slow and casual.

As relaxed and premodern as our work ways were, Pap and Mom represented exceptions. Pap had long been recognized in the extended Rader family circle as something of a workaholic. In the 1950s, he not only held down a job in town as an electrician that required his presence forty-four hours a week, but when the weather permitted, he toiled long, exhausting hours after work and on weekends on a wide range of projects extending from making improvements on our house to fixing fences. Mom was equally prone to hard work; she toiled from early in the morning until night doing housework, gardening, and rearing six children. The examples of our parents surely influenced the work ethic of Mike and me.

But unlike most farm boys in the Ozarks, we as teenagers worked without direct adult supervision. While Pap was in the background making plans for the work that he wanted done, he was rarely present or able to participate himself, even in the ordinary routines of milking cows and feeding livestock, let alone in plowing fields or putting up hay. Mom was nominally responsible for ensuring that Mike and I carried out Pap's plans, but her supervision was minimal; she was too busy caring our four younger siblings and doing routine household chores. Hence, in respects both large and small, Mike and I became in effect our own bosses. We learned at an exceptionally early age how to take charge of our own work, a skill that I think served both of us well in later life.

~

This having been said, Wichita introduced us to a strikingly different work experience. At the soda bottling plant, I found myself chained to a clock and what might be described as an assembly line consisting of a machine that cleaned and filled the bottles with soda. In the fall of 1953, I continued working half-time at Royal Crown while enrolled in classes at the University of Wichita. Lured by the prospect of much better pay, at the beginning of 1954, I began working forty hours a week for the Boeing Aircraft Company as a jig builder. At the same time, I continued to attend classes as a part-time student at the university. In the spring of 1954, Mike, who had returned to West Plains to finish his senior year in high school, rejoined me in Wichita. We soon moved out of the Eddings basement and rented an apartment in north Wichita.

A TYPICAL DAILY SCHEDULE OF MY LIFE AS A JIG MAKER

1:30 a.m. End of night shift at Boeing
2:30 a.m. Go to bed
7:00 a.m. Awaken, breakfast
8:00 a.m. English 101, University of Wichita
9:00 a.m. Western Civilization 101

10:00 a.m. One-hour break
11:00 a.m. Economics 101
12:00 p.m. Lunch
1:00 p.m. Nap? Study?
4:30 p.m. Begin night shift at Boeing

The next two and a half years were not for the faint of heart, at least not for me. My night-shift job at Boeing's immense aircraft plant required my arrival at four thirty in the afternoon and my departure at one thirty in the morning five days a week. It was not assembly-line work—that is, I did not actually build airplanes. Instead, after one month of training in reading blueprints, doing elementary trigonometry, and learning how to use various tools, I began working in Boeing's jig-building shop. (To mass-produce the mostly huge B-52 bombers for the US Air Force required specific jigs designed by aircraft engineers.)

During the week, I had virtually no free time. After getting off work at 1:30 a.m., I tried to snag a few hours of sleep before arriving on the university campus for classes. As often as not, my first class met at eight o'clock in the morning. Sometimes I was able take a quick nap before going to work in the afternoon, but classes often required homework, something incidentally I had done in study hall in high school. I loved most of my courses, especially the ones in history. I was fortunate to have as my instructor during the first semester in Western civilization Emory Lindquist, a Rhodes Scholar. (Later, he would serve as dean of the arts and sciences college and as president of the university.) Rarely if ever again would I hear lectures of such soaring elegance. It may have been then that I began to entertain a remote dream of becoming a history professor myself.

But I paid a price for holding down a well-paying full-time job at Boeing and simultaneously trying to be a successful student at the University of Wichita. It was not only the relentless schedule that was so difficult but also the fact that I had never before been lonelier. Having in the past been in a large family that included five siblings and ample quantities of free time, I suddenly found myself without the time to cultivate friendships with young people of my own age. Dating the opposite sex virtually did not exist. Living with my brother Mike offered only some relief, for he too had an arduous schedule which frequently included work on weekends.

After two and a half years, I finally extracted myself from this regimen. Not carrying a full academic load, lurking in the background was the possibility of being drafted into military service and in the foreground was the fact that I had saved up some $3,000 from my work at Boeing. Either I had to volunteer for military duty or seek a draft exemption by becoming a full-time student. I chose the latter. In the summer of 1956, I quit work at Boeing. As I left the plant with my toolbox in hand at one thirty in the morning of my final day of work, I consciously reminded myself of why I was quitting. I have rarely looked back since then.

As demanding as this experience was, I owe Wichita and Boeing more than I thought at the time. There was of course the money and the success of the university in stoking my affection for ideas and history. But even more important, as with many other Ozarkers who migrated into more highly regimented jobs elsewhere, it metaphorically case-hardened my personality. (Case-hardening refers to a process of hardening the surface of a metal so that it is more resistant to wear, bending, and breakage.) No longer was I simply a farm boy. Wichita had strengthened my capacity for coping with a world quite different from that of the warm and friendly confines of my own family and my Ozarks neighborhood.

In 1957, I returned to the Ozarks to attend Southwest Missouri State College, which had a cheaper tuition than Wichita, and became a full-time student. In 1958, I obtained a BA degree in history. That fall, I began graduate work in history that culminated in a PhD degree from the University of Maryland in 1964. In 1961, I married Barbara Koch.

PART IV

Are We in the Ozarks Now?

In the late 1960s and in the 1970s, my wife, two children, and I routinely vacationed in the Ozarks. Just about every summer, we loaded up a used car of dubious reliability and drove from our home in Lincoln, Nebraska, some five hundred miles southeastwardly, to my family's farm outside of West Plains, Missouri.

Once we had departed the tree-shaded streets of Lincoln, we found ourselves in the open vistas of the rolling countryside of southeastern Nebraska. Along the way, the trees were few and far between—clumps here and there on creek and river bottoms. On occasion, you could still view New Deal hedgerows or, more often, trees planted around houses and barns by the local farm families to shield themselves from the brisk winds that routinely swept across the plains. In the fields, we saw acre after acre of row crops—of corn, soybeans, and at that time, milo.

Some four hours later and two hundred miles down the road, we came upon the sprawling metropolis of Kansas City. In the earliest days of our annual vacations in the Ozarks, no multilane, limited access freeways sliced through or around the city. Every few blocks, we came to a full stop; traffic lights and traffic jams tested our patience. Once we had arrived on the other side of the city, we relaxed a little. For then, we found ourselves again in a rural/small-town landscape not too different from what we had left behind in southeastern Nebraska.

As we continued toward Springfield, Missouri, we began to sense that something had changed, that somewhere along the way we had crossed

Figure 20. Rader family, 1969. Left to right: daughter (Anne), son (Stephen, now deceased), wife (Barbara), and husband (Ben) visiting the family farm in the Schneider neighborhood of Howell County, Missouri. Courtesy of the author.

a mysterious boundary. Nothing officially announced our arrival in the Ozarks; there were no highway signs or guards examining our luggage or demanding to see our passports. Still, when we stopped at a café for lunch or at a filling station for gas, we noticed that the people talked a little differently than they did back in Lincoln—not so much the tongue of Shakespeare, as some scholars have claimed is characteristic of the Ozarks, but a slower, more muffled speech that included unusual verbal conjugations and unfamiliar pronunciations. For example, on one occasion after we had arrived in West Plains, Barbara announced that she needed to buy some "bells" for our daughter's shoes. Baffled by what Barbara had said, my teenaged sister Ada asked her to repeat it twice. Ada finally got it right. She blurted out, "Oh, you mean 'bales,'" as if Barbara were referring to bales of hay.

The scenery along the highway also subtly changed. No longer did we routinely see immaculate farmsteads of manicured yards, picket fences, and red-painted barns. As often as not, or so it seemed, we witnessed rusting farm machinery and abandoned cars propped up with rocks in the front yard. Untrimmed weeds, grass, and shrubs surrounded many of the farmsteads. Little wonder that Barbara wondered if there were any zoning laws in the Ozarks.

Of course, much of what we saw was not unique to the Ozarks. In many places in the America of that day, when driving across the country, you had to slow down and inch your way at twenty-five or thirty miles per hour through strings of small towns. In those days, there were no Walmart or Dollar General stores. Along the highway as you approached these small towns, a phalanx of billboards greeted you. Most of these signs hawked consumer goods or the availability of local services while others informed you that "JESUS SAVES!" When you turned on your car radio, you were as likely as not to hear an evangelical preacher holding forth on the wages of sin or pleading for money.

Today, these features of the Ozarks are not as conspicuous as they once were. Maybe it is partly a matter of speed; when hurtling down a mostly level interstate highway at seventy-five miles per hour, you are less likely to take notice of the changing terrain. You catch only brief glimpses of your surroundings. When low on fuel, rather than stopping at a filling station, just as you would do in the remainder of the nation, you pull off the highway onto a huge concrete island that features a convenience store. At that store, pumping gas is secondary to selling food, drinks, and dozens of other commodities. The bathrooms are likely to be cleaner. Even in the Ozarks, rarely do you see today rusting farm machinery or junked cars in front yards. Maybe you will even have difficulty detecting an unusual dialect. Spurred on by mass consumption and the mass media, the nationalization of sights and sounds continues to erase some of the Ozarks' uniqueness.

There are other reasons to think of the Ozarks and the Upland South in homogeneous terms. Take, for example, politics. Until the end of the twentieth century, the Civil War and Reconstruction had stamped the future political preferences of each county in different directions. Pro-Confederacy Shannon County had been reliably Democratic while pro-Unionist Howell had usually favored the Republican Party. In recent times, however, the Republicans have won smashing victories in both places. As recently as 1992, Bill Clinton, a Democrat, carried both counties, but by 2020, Donald Trump, a Republican, swamped Joe Biden, even in Shannon County, with more than 80 percent of the popular vote. Such results were not unique to these counties. Trump won resounding majorities throughout the Ozarks, the Upland South, and indeed, across rural and small-town America generally. Although far from conclusive, students of American politics have identified a bundle of cultural issues revolving around education, resentment of elites, race, gender, abortion, and religion that seem to explain these recent triumphs.

As in the Ozarks more generally, both counties suffer from high rates of poverty. For the 2015–19 era, their residents earned less than half the national per-capita income, though Howell countians did make about $4,000 more than Shannon's $17,387. For the same time frame, the Census Bureau found that nearly one-quarter of the residents in each county lived in poverty. Anecdotal and statistical evidence suggests that drug abuse, particularly of prescription opiates and methamphetamines, was unusually high in both counties. No one has illuminated the plight of the poor in this section of the Ozarks more vividly than novelist Daniel Woodrell, who happens to reside in West Plains. In particular, his novel *Winter's Bone* (2007), upon which a widely acclaimed film by the same name was based, brought to life the story of an intrepid teenaged girl who struggles to keep her family intact under the most adverse of circumstances.

In neither county do the farmers any longer plant much corn, nor in Howell County do very many farmers milk cows. Neither do the Shannon County farmers grow watermelons. The social fabric of the rural neighborhoods is no longer the same. Not since the 1950s has the Mahans Creek neighborhood of my youth had a post office, a country store, two churches, or a school. With the closure of the one-room school at Delaware, "we lost the social and focal point of our community," lamented one of my cousins, Thelma (Pummill) Winterbottom, who had once been a student and later a teacher there.[1] Although the Berean Baptist Church continues to hold regular services in the Schneider neighborhood of Howell County, its one-room school closed its doors permanently in 1959. The yellow school buses on the roads in both counties are only one of several indicators of a fundamental reorientation of the daily lives of the residents from the countryside to the nearby towns. In both counties, more countrypeople work in town than in the past.

~

In other respects, however, the histories of the respective counties have followed divergent trajectories. For decade after decade since World War II, Shannon County's population has stagnated at about eight thousand while in the last decade, the number of people in the Delaware Township (the Mahans Creek neighborhood) has plunged from nearly two hundred to only sixty-two people.

As with several smaller towns in the late twentieth-century Ozarks, small apparel factories, such as the one in Eminence, offered low-paying jobs to mostly women.[2] Although frequently divided about how to go about it, local civic boosters have also sought to transform the river areas of Shannon County into a tourist mecca. But located far away from a major population center (such as Springfield), their success has paled beside that of Branson, Missouri. The recent appearance of Casey and Dollar General convenience stores has contributed to the disappearance of the old-fashioned small-town grocery, gas, drug-, and hardware stores in Shannon County.

In the meantime, Howell County, in particular its county seat of West Plains and the nearby countryside, has witnessed a steady population growth.[3] In 2010, the Census Bureau even went so far as to classify the town and its surroundings (specifically Howell County) as one of the nation's micropolitan statistical areas. The word "micropolitan," echoing as it does the word "metropolitan," even evokes images of a big city rather than a small town. By 2010, more than forty thousand people, an increase from twenty-two thousand in 1960, resided in Howell County. Likewise, even the rural township of Sisson, where members of my family have resided on farms for some three generations, has increased by more than two hundred residents since 1960.

Although the soil is not rich by the standards of the corn belt to the north, its flatter land with a clay subsoil made it more suitable for growing row crops as well as cattle, hog, and dairy farming than most of Shannon County. A decisive turning point in the county's history came in 1883, when the railroad came to West Plains; local farmers could then ship their produce cheaply to either Springfield or Memphis, and the local merchants in turn could import goods to town more cheaply from elsewhere. West Plains itself quickly emerged as the largest trading center within a hundred-mile radius; it remains so to this day. After World War II, small dairy operations and raising feeder pigs flourished. In the 1960s and 1970s, West Plains even boasted that it was the "Feeder Pig Capital of the World." Since then, with the introduction of fescue to replace lespedeza as the standard pasture and hay crop in the region, most of the farmers have turned to growing grass-fed beef. In many cases, husband, wife, or both have supplemented the family's farm income by taking jobs in town.

In the meantime, the West Plains economy experienced fundamental changes as well. The town lost two of its major employers, the cheese and shoe manufacturing plants. The arrival in 1969 of mass retailer Walmart severely damaged the monopoly on trade once enjoyed by the old-line downtown merchants located mostly around the courthouse square. Town leadership began to shift away from these merchants and the local banks to a new, younger group of civic leaders. The new leaders boldly began to seek out (sometimes with the promise of subsidies) new kinds of enterprise, especially in the knowledge industries such as education, medicine, and the law.

Topping the list of new enterprises has been the development of the Ozarks Health Center, a sprawling complex that consists today of a 114-bed hospital that employs more than 1,200 people, including more than 100 primary care physicians and specialists in orthopedics, cardiology, oncology, and mental health. At the center, bragged the website of a local cardiology practice in 2022, you can even get open-heart surgery and "everything in between."

Next to the medical center in importance is Missouri State University–West Plains. Founded in 1963, today it employs a full-time faculty of about thirty plus some eighty part-time instructors. Not the least of its contributions to the area is its nursing program. From Howell and surrounding counties nearly two thousand full- and part-time students attend the two-year institution. In addition, West Plains constructed a new civic center that included an indoor pool and fitness center, eleven meeting rooms, and an arena seating thirty-five hundred spectators.

As with others, my own extended family has shared some of Howell County's relative bounty. Until his retirement to the farm in 1965, West Plains provided Pap with reliable cash-paying jobs as an electrician. Expanding on the electrical business established by Pap in 1956 and seizing on the opportunities occasioned by school consolidations and increased federal spending to upgrade public services in southcentral Missouri, my younger brother Mike became a highly successful building and public works contractor. At various times, my two youngest brothers, Leslie and Howard, worked for him. One of my sisters, Ada (and her husband, Mike), earned a comfortable living from sales and running beef cattle while my youngest sister (Alice) became a career teacher in the area's high schools. Of the six offspring of Lowell and Lydia Rader, only I, the oldest one, permanently left the Ozarks.

In sum, the recent history of these two counties bear striking resemblances to that of many other parts of Greater Appalachia and rural small-town America more generally. Poverty and dysfunctional families remain widespread due in part to the migration of well-paying jobs overseas as well as the decline of extractive industries. But there are other towns and cities scattered throughout the area, such as West Plains, that have prospered from jobs provided by becoming retail trade centers and by creating jobs in the knowledge industry. Still others have become tourist and food processing centers.

Indeed, northwestern Arkansas with its Tyson Foods, Walmart headquarters, and the University of Arkansas leading the way ranks among the more affluent places in the United States. Spectacularly representative of the new, nonrural image of the Ozarks is the Crystal Bridges Museum of American Art in Bentonville, Arkansas, which features not only a stunning building located in the woods but also a renowned collection of art ranging from Norman Rockwell to Andy Warhol.

That most of my kinfolk have remained in the Ozarks suggests the allure of the region for other reasons. That the cost of living in both Howell and Shannon Counties is some 20 percent below the national average offsets to some extent their pervasive social dysfunctionalities. Comparatively, housing costs and tax rates are especially low. The weather is usually mild. As Pap once perceptively observed, it was much more difficult to be homeless in the cold, windswept winters of Nebraska than it was in the warmer winters of southern Missouri.

And there remains to this day the Ozarks people and its scenery. The rolling hills, the verdant forests, and the clear-water fast-moving streams. Perhaps stunned by its primitive beauty, Congress in 1964 exempted a corridor along Jacks Fork–Upper Current River waterways in Shannon and nearby Carter County from private development. Few places like it exist anywhere in the United States. And for those who wish to step back in time or step aside from modern America's jolting quest for wealth and conquest, both counties offer something of a haven. For although one can obtain electricity and usually online computer service almost anywhere in either county, life there is a bit less hurried and intense than it is elsewhere.

The three vignettes that follow treat aspects of my relationship to the Ozarks after I permanently left the region in 1959.

34

"And I Was the Only Sober One in the Group"

This time, Mom took charge. Usually, she deferred to Pap; she ratified plans originating with him and did her best to aid him in their subsequent execution. But not in 1961, when she learned that I was to be married in far-off Riverdale, Maryland, a suburb of Washington, DC. Something about the prospect of traveling there prompted her to seize control. Nothing could stop her.

Maybe this departure from her previous behavior sprang from her age; she was forty-six years old and had never been so far away from the Ozarks before. Perhaps without telling anyone about it, she had long dreamed of visiting the nation's capital. And remember, as I revealed to you in an earlier vignette, even as a child up in McHenry Holler, she had become addicted to reading romantic novels.

In any case, her plan rested on research and lots of it. She obtained and pored over the road maps of each of the states through which she expected the family to pass. She gathered a stack of splashy promotional literature generated by state and local tourist information offices. Above all else, she read everything she could about the nation's capital city. She spent hours considering which of Washington's unique sites the family should visit.

As far as family members can remember, the trip met her expectations and more. Five of them loaded into a late-1950s Chevrolet driven by Howard, one of my younger brothers who had recently graduated from high school. They made their way across Missouri's bootheel, ferried the Mississippi River into Kentucky, visited Mammoth Cave, and crossed over the Blue Ridge Mountains into Virginia before finally arriving in the Washington, DC area. Escorted by me since I was at the time a graduate student at the nearby University of Maryland in College Park, they visited many of the standard tourist sites. Finally, they watched me get married to Barbara Koch at the Riverdale Presbyterian Church.

A sidenote: My family sensed that some of Barbara's kinfolk were unusual, but neither they nor I knew that among the witnesses of the wedding ceremony was a wide-eyed twelve-year-old cousin of Barb's, Maria Luisa Venegas Laguens, from Seville, Spain. Barb's mother, Clara, had been born in Spain, and Maria Luisa was living in the household of one of Clara's sisters while attending school in the United States. To Maria Luisa, the very Protestant ceremony was stark in its simplicity, but even more astonishing to her was the absence of drinking and dancing at the affair. Many years later, Maria Luisa, who would become a professor of English literature at the University of Seville and a close friend of ours, told us about her stunned reaction. Marriage in a Presbyterian church, eating cake, and drinking coffee afterward hardly approximated the boisterous celebratory culture surrounding a Spanish wedding.

Be that as it may, the Washington trip failed to sate Mom's curiosity about far-off places. Quite the contrary, it whetted her appetite for more. It was only the beginning over the next few years of a whirlwind of travel—to states adjacent to Missouri, to the homes of her grown children in North Carolina, Georgia, Texas, and Nebraska, to San Francisco to visit a sister dying from cancer, to England and Scotland, and to Canada, New England, and New York City, among other places. I know virtually nothing about the details of most of these trips, but I do have vivid memories of two long trips that she took with Barbara and me.

First and perhaps foremost was the trip to the British Isles. When I had received an invitation to make a presentation at an international sports history conference in Glasgow, Scotland in 1985, Barbara and I invited Mom to join us in doing a motor tour of England and Scotland. Mom did not hesitate; she not only accepted but also entered into a rigorous preparatory mode that would have been the envy of a would-be Olympic athlete. Upon learning that we had bought tickets to see *Troilus and Cressida* at the Royal Shakespeare Theatre at Stratford-upon-Avon, she set about reading this complex play based on Homer's *Illiad*. In addition, she literally went into physical training; each day, she walked from her house to the mailbox and back, about a mile altogether. "I have to be ready," she explained to her daughters, "for the walking that Ben and Barbara will demand of me." (In fact, Barbara, sympathetic to the rigors of walking the uneven medieval streets for long distances, devised a plan that relieved Mom of much of the physical duress by having her take a seat while we scouted out potential eating places, sites, and the like.)

Far from being anticlimactic, the trip itself more than fulfilled her dreams. Carefully keeping a detailed diary of her experiences, she got to see and tour London itself, to see Salisbury's spectacular Gothic cathedral, Stonehenge, the well-preserved medieval walls of Chester, remnants of Hadrian's Wall, and so on. When driving across the countryside, we scheduled each morning a new bed and breakfast for the evening. Several of these were not England's best, but they frequently offered unusual opportunities to meet and talk to locals.

She discovered fish and chips, taverns, and that her firstborn son drank alcoholic beverages! The fish and chips, sometimes wrapped in newspapers, varied in quality. The ubiquitous pubs served as sites for lunches and dinners. We did not learn about her reaction to them until near the end of our trip when we were touring near the white cliffs of Dover. When eating lunch in a countryside pub featuring unusually rich walnut and oak paneling, she observed that she had never expected to find such establishments to be so elegant. What she thought about me having a glass of wine or a beer with dinner, she never disclosed—at least to me. I am also thinking that even though a lifelong teetotaler, she never mentioned this aspect of the trip to those eager listeners back in the Ozarks whom she regaled with her stories of adventure.

But this reticence, provided that that is what it was, changed during a long circular trip that we made with her up through eastern Canada, down through New England to New York City, to Barbara's kinfolk in the Washington, DC area, then on to see a granddaughter in North Carolina, before finally arriving back in the Ozarks. At Newport, Rhode Island, we met longtime former colleagues (John Cullen and Jean Johnson) who were then teaching at the University of Rhode Island. The Cullens invited us to dine with them at a seafood restaurant located on a fishing scow anchored in Newport's harbor.

When we got back to West Plains, I seized on the opportunity to tell the rest of the family a story. I explained that while the five of us were exiting the boat, Mom had tripped and fallen on the scow's gangplank. She then surprised both Barbara and me by adding, "And yes, I was the only sober one in the group!"

35

Barbara Learns about High Finance in the Ozarks

My wife, Barbara, is not an Ozarker. Far from it! She is a product of the Washington, DC suburbs. And as I mentioned earlier, her mother had been born in Seville, Spain, and her father was a second-generation

Figure 21. Barbara Koch Rader, my wife, about 1970. Courtesy of the author.

German American born in Baltimore. Not surprisingly given his ethnicity, her father carefully managed the family's finances. From an early age, Barbara remembered watching him meticulously examine and balance his checkbook at the end of each month. Indeed, for many years, he carried on a running dispute with his local bank, for he claimed that it had made a one-cent error in its own favor!

Well, needless to say, Barbara, along with the rest of her immediate family, experienced something of a cultural shock when she became involved with me. She loves to tell the story about when we were courting and she was at my apartment when I received my mail. One of the items in my mail was a statement from my bank, which I ripped open. After a brief and casual examination, I said, "That's about what I thought I had in the bank" and then proceeded to throw the statement into a nearby wastebasket. At that moment, though she said nothing, Barbara remembers thinking, "If I marry this guy, I am going to take charge of the money!"

Not long after this incident, we drove more than a thousand miles from the Washington, DC suburbs to West Plains, Missouri so that I could introduce my exotic fiancée to my parents. I had only one problem: As a penniless graduate student, I had no money for an engagement ring. My generous mother responded that the family would raise the money by selling a cow, the usual method for the family to meet unexpected demands for cash. Upon the sale of the cow, Barbara witnessed an equally vivid example of Ozarker high finance. Rather than recording the amount of the transaction in a checkbook or in a family account book (which the family did not have), my mom wrote down the amount on the back of an envelope, which she then placed on top of other envelopes containing family financial data.

Recently, I gave some additional thought to the family's casual financial recordkeeping. In the first place, I recognized that at least one side of the family (the Raders rather than the Pummills) had long prized a dilatory way of life that subordinated money to other values. And in the second place, that on a day-to-day basis, my own family while living on Mahans Creek had for the most part been in a cashless economy—that is, neither Pap nor Mom received regular cash incomes, that they consumed much of what they produced, that they bartered for some needed items, or that they sold some eggs, butter, or perhaps a cow when they had to have cash. In short, they had little need to keep careful financial records.

In some respects, all of that changed when Pap took a job as an electrician in West Plains. He normally deposited his weekly paycheck in a local bank. Henceforth, my family used checks to pay for almost everything; this included the weekly grocery bill, the irregular purchase of hardware items, livestock, farm equipment, and so forth. Although Pap sometimes forgot to report to Mom a check that he had written, she tried as best she could to keep a running tab of the checks by recording them on the back of used envelopes. This unorthodox bookkeeping system apparently worked, for the most part, pretty well. I should also observe that in time, the family even filled out a long 1040 income tax form that included farm expenses deductions. Exactly how they calculated these, I do not know.

~

But I digress. The sale of the cow in order to purchase an engagement ring was not the final lesson of Barbara's education in Ozarks finance. Although Pap never explicitly said so, he harbored a dream that someday in the future, his children, their spouses, and his grandchildren would live near the family farm outside of West Plains. In short, he wanted to replicate the geographic clustering of kinfolk as the Childress clan had done back in Hart County, Kentucky and the Rader-Pummills had done down on Mahans Creek. Consistent with this plan, he began in his later years to purchase land adjacent to the family farm on which he imagined that one of his children would someday build a house or, at the least, live in a trailer house. To a rather surprising extent, his plan succeeded, for three of my five siblings did precisely that, settling on the family farm or on land adjacent to it.

Consistent with his plan, Pap sought to lure me, whom he described as his Prodigal Son, back to the family's network of nearby farms. (At this time, with my own family of a wife and two small children, I was a professor of history at the University of Nebraska.) To accomplish this, he proposed to us the idea of buying eighty acres of the old Vaughn place. The farm was adjacent to the home place, on a paved county road, and as Pap observed, the price of the land was sure to increase. Furthermore, we could deduct expenses incurred from owning the land from our income taxes and we could borrow the money to pay for it from one of the local banks. Pap would cosign the loan. Why Barbara and I agreed to this plan is unclear. As it was, we were barely balancing the family budget and neither of us had any intention of moving down to an Ozarks farm. Given the rapid inflation of the 1970s, perhaps we thought the purchase might be a good way to help finance our children's college educations.

In any case, at the First National Bank on the West Plains square, we met with the president to sign the legal documents (including the loan) connected with the purchase of the old Vaughn farm. Upon completion of the signing, Barbara, who had indeed taken charge of my own family's finances, finally expressed her fears openly if indirectly: "What is the monthly payment for this loan?" she blurted out.

The bemused bank president smiled and drawled, "Well, when you have a little extra money, you can send some of it to us."

Later on, Barbara said that this banking experience gave her a better understanding of the Whitewater scandal. By the way, I am reasonably sure that this kind of highly personal banking practice no longer exists in the Ozarks. Indeed, nearly all the banks in the region today are members of branch-banking systems with headquarters located elsewhere. I presume these banks follow far more formal banking procedures.

36

I Took Her Hands in Mine

Upon returning to Nebraska from a European vacation in 1991, Barbara and I spent the night in Omaha with our daughter Anne. As a medical school student there, Anne knew well the insidious nature of cancers. She reported that my mom had a colon cancer that had metastasized. The grim conclusion: Mom did not have long to live. As soon as we could get things in order, we drove from Lincoln down to the family farm to see Mom. She had just completed an operation that entailed the removal of some of her colon, and she seemed in reasonably good spirits.

It fell upon me to accompany her on the follow-up visit with the young oncologist who had performed the operation. Upon entering the examination room, the doctor sat in front of her on a stool and took her hands in his. His face revealed the gravity of the situation. Nearly in tears, he reported the results. The operation was not successful. The cancer had spread far beyond her colon. No one cried, but had we been other than Ozarkers, perhaps we would have.

After the examination, we got into my car to go pick up a pizza for supper that evening. Before driving away, I thought I should say something appropriate but what? In many respects, Mom had had a tough life. She had birthed six children between 1935 and 1949. Most of that time, she had spent rearing the children alone on isolated farms.

Memories, mostly of regret, flashed by. Had she lived the life that she had dreamed of as a youngster? I remembered that upon graduation from Eminence High School, she had planned to teach in a local one-room school. She had successfully taken the county's teaching exam, but because of the exigencies of the Great Depression, there were no jobs. She married my father instead.

I took her hands in mine and unaccountably blurted out, "Have I had the life that you dreamed of?" She responded with an emphatic yes! I at once felt guilty and have remained so ever since.

I then started the car, and we drove off to the pizza parlor.

EPILOGUE
The Ozarks of the American Imagination

One cool, spring morning in 1946, my uncle Hulbert "Hub" Rader walked up the steep hill to retrieve the family's mail. As he approached the mailbox on Highway E, a Chevrolet sedan pulled up beside him. Occupying the car was none other than the enormously popular radio comedians Fibber McGhee and Molly, who, as it happened, were taking their vacation in the Ozarks. Rolling down the passenger-side car window, Molly said to Hub, "Excuse us, where can we find a real hillbilly?" Without missing a beat, his ubiquitous pipe in hand and a twinkle in his eye, Hub responded, "You're looking at one right now!" Upon completion of telling this story, Uncle Hub broke into laughter. For, once again, an allegedly unsophisticated Ozarker had bested a couple of "city slickers."

While it may have been difficult for Fibber McGhee and Molly to recognize a real hillbilly when they saw one, this was not the case with my son-in-law, Ken Gatter, who is from upscale Westchester County, New York. Shortly after his marriage in 1987 to my daughter, Anne, she convinced Ken that he should meet her great-uncle Hub. As they got out of their car at the old Rader farm, up walked Hub dressed in overalls without a shirt or an undershirt on and a double-barreled shotgun slung over his shoulder. With some trepidation, Ken concluded at once that he was in the presence of a genuine hillbilly. As if to confirm his conclusion, Uncle Hub and Aunt Wilma then proudly displayed to Ken and Anne their ingenuity. When adding a new room to the back of their house, rather than removing a tree stump located in the middle of the new room, they simply nailed a new homemade tabletop to the top of the stump.

Just as in the cases of Ken Gatter and Fibber McGhee and Molly, in the American imagination, the cartoonlike version of the "hillbilly" jumps out ahead of all others as a descriptor of a unique way of life attributed to the residents of the Upland South. It is a staple of popular culture. Novelists like Harold Bell Wright, country musicians like Dolly Parton, and television sitcoms like *The Beverly Hillbillies* have woven a romantic shroud of fantasy and nostalgia around the idea of the hillbilly. As often as not, the shroud brought together sharply opposing images of the denizens of southern Appalachia and the Ozarks.

One powerful constituent of the stereotype is the alleged backwardness of hillbillies. Stated bluntly, they are said to be out of step with modern times. They (are) were a more primitive people, perhaps sharing qualities commonly attributed to Native Americans or perhaps South Sea islanders. They live in impermanent log cabins or perhaps trailer houses, spend much of their time hunting, fishing, or loafing, form family clans, drink corn whiskey, and are especially sensitive about their honor. They train their male children to become warriors. Even their religion is filled with bombast and violent metaphors. Not happy converts to the Protestant work ethic, they tend to be lazy and poor.

On the positive side of the hillbilly dichotomy is its alleged simplicity. Hillbillies value the "common sense" of "granny" wisdom more than the sophisticated learning of scholars. Absent from their lives is the single-minded pursuit of wealth and conquest of modern America; they are satisfied to live in the warm cocoon of family and neighborhood. Absent from their lives is an obsession with time; unlike other Americans, they are more driven by the imperatives of the moment than by the ticking clock. Absent from their lives is a genuflection to the hierarchies required by those who are seeking success in modern America. Unpretentious, hillbillies defer to no one. Living simply is a precondition of happiness. In this almost arcadian setting, there is less anxiety, less fear, and less deceit. Throughout the twentieth and extending into the twenty-first centuries, critics of modernity, especially those in literary and artistic circles, have found inspiration in this alternative of the imagined hillbilly.

As the vignettes in this book suggest, the main problem with the idea of the hillbilly is its vast oversimplification. For every instance of poverty attributable to lazy, hard-drinking, drug-taking malingerers, there are even more instances of poverty springing from the absence of opportunity. Not all parts of the Ozarks are identical. Even adjacent counties such as Shannon and Howell in Missouri have in their recent histories evolved in opposing directions. Although far from becoming a true and homogeneous arcadia, the Ozarks, like the remainder of rural and small-town America, requires an understanding in more complex terms than that of the hillbilly. Let us hope that this little book has contributed to that cause.

NOTES

PREFACE

1. See David D. Gilmore, "Some Notes on Community Nicknaming in Spain," *Man* 17 (December 1982): 686–700, https://www.jstor.org/stable/2802040.

PART I. THE CLEAR, COLD WATER OF MAHANS CREEK

1. Quoted in Benjamin G. Rader, *Down on Mahans Creek: A History of an Ozarks Neighborhood* (Fayetteville: University of Arkansas Press, 2017), vii.

2. Terry G. Jordan-Bychkov, *The Upland South: The Making of a Folk Region and Landscape* (Santa Fe: Center for American Places, 2003), 1–5.

3. Notes from a telephone interview with Ivy (Eddings) Shumate by the author, August 13, 2012. Copy in possession of author.

4. For the transition of courtship practices in Shannon County, see Benjamin G. Rader, "'My Girl' Bill French Goes a Courtin': The Old and the New in Missouri Ozarks Courtships, 1908–1913," *Missouri Historical Review* 109 (July 2015): 254–67.

5. See https://www.care.com/c/born-with-a-veil-what-it-means/ (March 15, 2022).

6. Hubert "Hub" Rader, "Edward Martin 'Sam' Rader," in Jayne Rader, "Rader Family 2002," 78, unpublished manuscript in possession of the author.

7. *The Passerby*, February 3, 1938, the Pummill family newsletter, a copy in possession of the author.

8. *Current Wave*, April 9, 1908.

9. J. Anderson Childress, *Beyond the Cross Roads: A Genealogy, History, and Traditional Folkways of Western Hart County, Kentucky* (Utica, KY: McDowell Publications, 1981), 43.

10. "In the Backwoods," in *The Literature of the Ozarks: An Anthology*, ed. Phillip Douglas Howerton (Fayetteville: University of Arkansas Press, 2019), 34.

PART II. THE PEOPLE THERE EVEN DRANK RAINWATER FROM CISTERNS

1. For a similar response in a place far removed from the Ozarks, see Jiarui Cao, Yiqing Xu, and Chuanchaun Zhang, "Clans and Calamity: How Social Capital Saved Lives during China's Great Famine," *Journal of Development Economics* 157 (2002): 1–14.

2. Jerome Rader, digitally recorded interview, October 13, 2009, and Arch Pummill, phone interview with the author, February 11, 2010.

3. "Record of Dist. #4, Township 25, Range 8, for School Year Beginning July 1, 1909, and Ending July 1, 1910," in *Schneider School Reunion, July 16, 1988: A Brief History of Schneider School*, comp. Don Smith (n.p.: [1988?]). Copy in possession of the author.

4. Quoted in http://www.rootsweb.ancestry.com/~moshanno/memory_lane.htm (March 9, 2022).

5. *The Passerby*, February 10, 1933.

PART III. "I WOULD CHOOSE TO LIVE IN TOWN OR BESIDE A BUSY COUNTY ROAD"

1. See "4-H Sunday," Extension Circular 0-49-2, http://digital commons.unl.edu.

2. Quoted in Mabel L. Cooper, *3-Rs in the Ozarks* (Eminence, MO: Chilton Publishing, 1980), 60.

3. As quoted in Benjamin G. Rader, *Down on Mahans Creek: A History of an Ozarks Neighborhood* (Fayetteville: University of Arkansas Press, 2017), 169.

4. https://mdc.mo.gov/discover-nature/field-guide/multiflora-rose/.

5. As quoted in Rader, *Down on Mahans Creek*, 141.

6. *Current Wave*, October 24, 1929.

7. For the massive outmigration of people from the Ozarks in the 1950s and 1960s, see Brooks Blevins, *A History of the Ozarks, Volume 3, The Ozarkers* (Urbana: University of Illinois Press, 2021), 219–24.

PART IV. ARE WE IN THE OZARKS NOW?

1. Thela Winterbottom, "Delaware School," *Ozarker*, August 1978, 9.

2. For the changing face of economic development in the late twentieth- and early twenty-first-century Ozarks, see especially Brooks Blevins, *A History of the Ozarks, Volume 3, The Ozarkers* (Urbana: University of Illinois Press, 2021), chap. 7.

3. In comparing Shannon and Howell Counties, I am particularly indebted to Kathleen Blakeny Morrison, "The Poverty of Place: A Comparative Study of Five Rural Counties in the Missouri Ozarks" (PhD diss., University of Missouri, 1999); Kathy Morrison to Benjamin Rader, December 16, 2021, email in possession of the author; telephone interview with Mike Rader, December 21, 2021.

BENJAMIN G. RADER is James L. Sellers Professor Emeritus of History at the University of Nebraska, Lincoln. His books include *Down on Mahans Creek: A History of an Ozarks Neighborhood* and *Baseball: A History of America's Game*, fourth edition.

The University of Illinois Press
is a founding member of the
Association of University Presses.

———————————————————

Composed in 11.5/14.5 Garamond Premier Pro
by Kirsten Dennison
at the University of Illinois Press
Manufactured by Sheridan Books, Inc.

University of Illinois Press
1325 South Oak Street
Champaign, IL 61820-6903
www.press.uillinois.edu